LAUGHTER IN QUAKER GREY

*William Haughton Sessions wrote this book in
1952 and it continues to sell steadily on both
sides of the Atlantic. William Sessions was born
in York in 1878, his lifetime spanning the reigns
from Victoria to Elizabeth. Only a few weeks
prior to his death at the age of 88 in 1966, he
was checking the proofs of his sequel* More
Quaker Laughter *published in 1967. In addition to developing and consolidating his printing
business, he was Treasurer of The Retreat Mental Hospital in York for more than thirty years.
A York City Councillor for 14 years as a young
man, he stood three times for Parliament as a
Liberal Candidate, was President of the British
Federation of Master Printers, Chairman of Bul-
mer Magistrates, and Chairman (later President)
of York City Football Club. From this long and
many-sided life he culled and savoured quaint
and quizzical sayings and happenings that are
the spice of life, always seeking humour which
explains and reconciles in preference to irony
or sarcasm which divides and hurts. It is this
philosophy which he shares with you in these pages.*

LAUGHTER
IN QUAKER GREY

Collected by

WILLIAM H. SESSIONS

WILLIAM SESSIONS LIMITED
YORK, ENGLAND

FIRST PUBLISHED : 1952

SECOND IMPRESSION : 1966

THIRD IMPRESSION : 1974
(WITH SMALL REVISIONS)

ISBN 0 900657 30 8

*Printed in Great Britain
by William Sessions, Limited
The Ebor Press, York.*

CONTENTS

ACKNOWLEDGEMENTS

I AM GRATEFUL to Friends from all over the world who have sent me stories. These have come in such numbers that to publish them all would make a massive tome, whereas a collection of stories seems to fit best into a smaller volume. I have therefore made a selection, hoping that if this proves of interest it may be possible to publish a further book of Quaker stories.

If therefore, dear Friend, thy story is not here, and thou thinkest it is a better one than some which appear, consider, that if another volume is to be published, I must keep back some of the best, which doubtless includes thine, to brighten up that other volume.

It has not been possible to mention all the names of the Friends who have sent the stories published here, but I should like to thank Ernest H. Bennis, of Limerick; Isabel Grubb, M.A., for the extracts from *Quakers in Ireland*; Horace Mather Lippincott, of Philadephia, Chairman of the Publications Committee of the American Friends' Historical Society; Ruth and Irwin Poley for extracts from *Quaker Anecdotes* published by Pendle Hill; and the *Boys Own Paper* for leave to publish "Pickled Cockles." The delightful poem "A Little Maiden's Gown" came to me in manuscript; I believe it has been published, but by whom I have been unable to discover.

Lastly, but by no means least, I have received much help from my wife, my son, my daughter E. Anne King and E. Philip Dobson.

W. H. SESSIONS

PREFACE

THE THINKING OF OUR TIME has again turned to the function of humour as being somehow related to that of religious faith. Humour, like religion, possesses a quality of forgiveness and understanding that reconciles us with the weaknesses of others and ourselves. It permits us to throw off our cares and worries and lends us the confidence that our defeats are only temporary. Irony is different. It acts haughtily and disciplines others. It stresses superiority over others and lacks the element of reconcilation that humour supplies. We laugh, and ought to laugh, about the incongruities of life; about the foibles of pretentious or vain people; about our own momentary confusions; about misunderstandings or grotesque situations. We also laugh about moments of real fear after they are over. The powers of life that are apt to oppress us are not infrequently overcome by humour.

But humour cannot solve the deeper problems of life. We cannot possibly imagine Jesus laughing at a sick man or sinner seeking His help. Humour cannot prepare in us a vision of things higher and more enduring than the life that surrounds us daily. It may clear away some of the debris of the past, but we need building material for the future. We must not be satisfied by merely removing the embarrassments of yesterday and escaping into the pseudo-humour of our comics. Perhaps it is more than a mere accident that the decline in organized religious activities noted in this generation went hand in hand with the mushroom growth of cheap humour in reading matter and films. We must learn to distinguish between humour and joy, the latter being the result of true inner harmony. But whatever both may do for us, only faith can brace us up against the serious perplexities of life. And only faith can give us the material out of which we may build an enduring structure for humanity's future.

"Friends Intelligencer" Editorial 1946
(with the English Spelling of "humour")

CHAPTER I

HUMOUR

I HAVE HESITATED about putting down a series of Quaker anas separated by a short line or five asterisks. (The plain line would be more Quakerly!) Such a continuous series of paragraphs, for page after page, grows tedious; it seems to want a frame to separate one picture of Quaker life from the other.

It is to give this framework that I have added wording of my own. What better master to follow than Shakespeare. He in his tragedies always brings in some lighter relief, so that the hearer can go back to the tragic situations with refreshed appreciation. I have reversed the position, and introduced the tragedy of my own wording, so that the reader can the more enjoy the story which follows!

I am most grateful to the many Friends from all parts of the world who have sent me stories, but I realise that a serious historian would find difficulty about some of them.

Here in these pages will be found but little in the historic manner with the original sources carefully recorded in a foot-note. For these stories have been handed down by word of mouth, as I have found from receiving the same story in different form from several correspondents. It is the point of the story which is remembered, the parts which clothe and illustrate this point are less accurately committed to memory, and so indeed often vary considerably from one teller to another.

Sometimes it is possible to check these lapses of memory concerning the less important details. Take this story, for example:—

The Owning of Huddersfield

Thomas Firth was considered "a character" even in that home of "characters," the West Riding of Yorkshire. Sir John Ramsden, desirous of owning all Huddersfield, had bought out all the freeholders of the town except for a cottage and small piece of land owned by Thomas Firth. Sir John made several tempting offers to the Quaker, and, on their being refused, finally said he would "cover the ground with sovereigns." Thomas Firth considered this, for it was very far beyond the real value of the property. Sir John waited hopefully, and then the Quaker said: "Put thy sovereigns on edge, friend Ramsden, and I will sell." Sir John snorted at this, and of course refused. "Then," said Thomas Firth, "thee and me will have to own Huddersfield between us."

This is the story I had heard several times, and it is well told by my correspondent, but later I received another version, which showed that the above story had grown in the telling. This later correspondent made Sir John say: "I will cover your *doorstep* with sovereigns." A little calculation shows that Sir John would offer anything between £200,000 and £500,000 for the cottage and small piece of land in the first story, an altogether improbable sum, especially considering the value of money at that time. Covering the broad doorstep of a country house makes the offer between £5,000 and £10,000, a much more likely amount.

In the above tale, arithmetic and land values enable the details of the story to be checked, but most often it is not possible to do this with two, or even more versions of a story. The teller then selects the one he likes best; indeed he may indulge in that very human desire to "improve" a tale; for these are told to amuse, not as historical records— After all *Punch* has long ago dropped putting "a fact" against a story. It is indeed a question how much the teller may be allowed "to improve" his tale. Take the case of hearing a story which is badly told, but the point of the story is rich in humour. Shall we reclothe the details a little better when we re-tell it?

Dr. John Watson, who wrote a delightful book on wit and humour, had this same point put to him. The Rev. John Watson, D.D., Minister of the Free Church of Scotland, considered the question with some perplexity for a few minutes. Then his love of a well-told story made him say, with a twinkle in his eye, "It depends how good the alteration is!" Was John Watson right? It depends surely on the point of the story. If the tale is of some historical fact, or to illustrate the character of a person, then it is necessary to try to remember the full details accurately. If the story is one told for the telling, to brighten the tedious hour, and it has been poorly told to us, then surely we can clothe it a little better—remembering

John Watson's dictum, that the alteration must be good.

I recognise I am on dangerous ground here in giving this advice; but we all know that the difference between a good teller of a tale and a poor one lies in the brief but skilful way in which the good storyteller clothes his tale, so that we picture the scene, the better to enjoy the point when it appears.

Falling Softly

Let me illustrate John Watson's "the alteration must be good" by the story of a weighty Friend—weighty in the Quaker and the avoirdupois senses—who had been involved in a stage-coach accident. He wrote home to say the coach had been overturned, but "All is well! I was favoured to fall on brother Josiah!"

The other version of the story is that a weighty visiting Friend rode to Meeting, and by the door was thrown from his horse. He wrote home that he was unhurt because he was "favoured to fall on a woman Friend!"

The first is the better version, because the hearer will not lose the point of the story through sympathy with the woman Friend; the unknown Josiah has less of our sympathies.

Here on the other hand is a story where the humour has been improved in another version, yet the first is a fact, whereas the second is not. What are we, lovers of plain speech to say to the second? I suggest, tell them both, the actual one first, saying, after the laughter has died down at the second one, that its correctness is more than doubtful. The first version is :—

Out-Queening the Queen

When George V and Queen Mary visited the Cadbury Chocolate Works, George and Elizabeth Cadbury showed them round. Going through the grounds the old Quaker led the way with the Queen, and his wife followed with the King. To show respect George Cadbury walked with his hat off. Fearing that he might catch cold the Queen reversed an earlier experience with royalty, and said, "Mr. Cadbury, please put on your hat." "Oh no, thank you," he replied. "Please, Mr. Cadbury," said the Queen, and added playfully, "if you do not I shall ask the King to command you." Still George Cadbury hesitated. At that moment Elizabeth Cadbury looked up, and said, "George, put on thy hat." He did so at once.

The other version of the story makes the King walking with George Cadbury and the Queen with Dame Elizabeth. There is the same play about the hat, and the King is made to say, "You are the older man, if you will not put on your hat, I must take off mine," which he did. Just then Elizabeth Cadbury looked up, and said in her most regal manner, "George, put on thy hat." Both Georges, King and subject, promptly put on their hats.

What too are we to say to those other stories which are frankly invented because of a trait in a Friend or in Quakers generally. I know the next one comes in this class, because the teller said afterwards he had thought it out on his way home that evening:—

Remembering a Face

Fielden Thorp, retired Head of Bootham School, came into a shop, and saw a lady whose face seemed familiar to him. Looking at her he said, "I seem to know thy face; what is thy name?" To which the lady replied, "Thou ought to know my face, seeing thee've been married to it for well over thirty years."

The reason we enjoyed this so much was because Fielden Thorp could never remember our names. He would invite us to tea on a Saturday, but when we went up to him after Sunday morning meeting to thank him, the familiar phrase always came, "I seem to know thy face; what is thy name?"

Stories too become associated with individuals, possibly because they fit, as in the above; but often because of inaccurate memory. Someone hears a story of "a Woman Friend in Quaker garb," and when repeating it associates it with possibly the last remaining "Quaker Bonnet" in his Meeting. Certainly in the days of my youth, fifty and more years ago, when Quaker dress for men had died out, and for women almost so, the following two stories were told about the last Friend in Quaker dress in almost every Meeting. In York it was associated with Elizabeth Gurney Dimsdale; in other Meetings it was with some other Friend.

The Cab and the Quakeress

A very old cab came to take the Quakeress to the station. She told the cabman he was late and he must hurry or she would miss her train. On the way the cab bottom dropped out, and the Quakeress had to run inside the cab to keep up with it. All her frantic signals to the driver were taken to mean signs to hurry faster. The more she knocked on the front window, the faster she had to run! The onlookers beheld a hurrying cab with the curious sight of grey Quaker stockings running beneath it. The story was told too at a time when it was considered dashing, if not "fast," to show even an ankle in crossing a muddy street.

The other story was:—

Meat to Eat

The Quakeress on a visit in the Service of Truth was pressed to eat more than she felt able, so she slipped some of the food into her pocket. At evening Meeting she rose to speak with the words, "I have meat to eat that ye know not of." Unthinkingly pulling out her handkerchief, the hidden food came out of her pocket, to emphasise unexpectedly her text.

In the parts of this book which have an historical background I have tried to make the stories as accurate as possible. My "cautionary tale" in this introduction is to say that in these stories there will be some which fall into one or other of the classes I have been discussing—the story where the point is correct, but the other details more or less inaccurate —the story where the point remains, but the background has been altered—the story which has been "improved"—and the story which has been invented. It is quite impossible to verify the actual facts which gave rise to the story, especially as some of the stories have been handed down from generation to generation for long years in the Society. Perhaps the best conclusion to the matter is: if the story is good and worth telling, let it cheer us on our way.

"In the Interest of Truth," I suggest that the point of a story is generally accurate, whilst the proneness of man to forget comes out in the details which clothe that point. After all such variations are in the true tradition of the motto we see every week on the cover of *The Friend*—"In essentials unity—in non-essentials liberty." I can but hope too that the reader, when thinking of the compiler, especially after coming across what is to him "a chestnut," will remember that this quotation ends—"in all things charity!"

It has to be remembered too that truth is stranger than fiction. There was one story which I really could not think had actually happened, in spite of it being told by Rufus Jones. I thought he must have used it as a parable, to encourage Friends to welcome a stranger even into their own special seat, instead of feeling some annoyance at their seat being taken. Here it is, and it well illustrates what I suggested before, that the point of the story is most often more accurate than the details:—

Two at Meeting

The graveyard and migration to the city finally reduced the rural Meeting to one member—a man who faithfully kept the Meeting going by unfailing but solitary attendance. One Sunday morning, as he walked up the aisle, he saw an unexpected visitor there ahead of him. He stopped and said, "Friend, thou art in my seat!"

I was interested therefore to receive this story from E. Vipont Brown, the very Friend who was asked to move.

"Thou art sitting in my Seat"

Many years ago I was cycling from Plymouth one Sunday morning, on my way home to Manchester. I intended to go to Meeting at Wellington, but I made good pace, and determined to go on to Taunton. At Taunton I asked my way to the Meeting House, and with great difficulty I found it. I was a little late, but I found a large Meeting House empty. However, I went in, and sat down to worship alone. Presently however, I heard a shuffling of feet, and an old Friend and his wife came in by separate doors. The old lady sat down on the women's side, and the old man walked up the aisle to where I was sitting and gently touched my shoulder, saying, "I am sorry to ask thee to move, but thou art sitting in my seat." Needless to say I moved up one, and we three worshipped together."

I am sometimes asked: what is the difference between wit and humour? Think for a moment of the pictures which come into the mind of "a wit" and "a humorist," the two will be very different. "Wit" carries a sting; "humour" is good fun.

Take the story "The Owning of Huddersfield." It will be agreed that, "Put thy sovereigns on edge" was a humorous way of declining to sell, but "Thee and me will have to own Huddersfield between us" was wit; it carried a very decided sting for the man whose ambition to own all Huddersfield had been thwarted.

This is borne out by Dr. John Watson ("Ian Maclaren") who says in his book on Humour, that wit is sharp, with a barbed point, whilst humour is broad, kindly and full of laughter. He also adds: "If you have a story which has fun in its telling, then suddenly ends with an unexpected turn of still better humour, treasure that story; it is a good one to tell."

It is not out of place to conclude this chapter with what two Quaker authors have written about George Fox's sense of humour.

Edward Grubb

"There are many indications in George Fox's *Journal* that, with all its gravity, he was not without a sense of humour. It must have been with an inward chuckle that he often confuted on their own principles the Bible worshippers of his day, who regarded every word of Scripture, even in the English Translation, as Divinely infallible—as when he 'reproved' certain people who 'held that women had no souls,' by quoting Mary's song (Luke 1.46), 'My soul doth magnify the Lord.' "

"A more amusing instance is in the Court at Launceston in Cornwall in 1656, where the Judge ordered Fox and a companion prisoner to take off their hats. Fox asked where in the Bible any such order had been given, and the Judge could only say, 'Take him away'. 'So they took us away, and put us among the thieves.' Presently after he called to the jailer, 'Bring them up again!' 'Come,' said he, 'where had they hats, from Moses to Daniel? Come, answer me, I have you fast now!' Fox replied, 'Thou mayst read in the third of Daniel, that the three children were cast in the fiery furnace by Nebuchadnezzar's command with their coats, their hose, *and their hats on*.' This plain instance stopped him, so that, not having anything else to say to the point, he cried again, 'Take them away, jailer'."

"Again, at Lancaster in 1664, Fox, who had a smattering of Hebrew, astonished the Court by exclaiming in a loud voice (when he had been ordered to take the Oath) 'Lotish shabmin becoll daker.' (Ye shall not swear by anything.) 'Whereupon,' he says, 'they all gazed, and there was a great calm'."

William C. Braithwaite

" 'Above all,' says Penn, 'George Fox excelled in prayer. The inwardness and weight of his spirit, the reverence and solemnity of his address and behaviour, and the fewness and fullness of his words, have often struck even strangers with admiration, as they used to reach others with consolation. The most awful, living reverent frame I ever felt or beheld, was his in prayer.'

"But this intimacy with the higher life made him at times a rare humorist, struck with the odd contradictions and confusions of the world about him. At

Lancaster, when tendered the oath, he held up the
Bible, as the book which forbade swearing, and said
he wondered that it was allowed liberty. At Tenby,
after he had racily argued the hat question, the
governor cried, 'Away with these frivolous things,'
and was met with the retort, 'Why then imprison
my friend for frivolous things?' When the Roman
Catholic governor groped his way into the smoky
room at Scarborough where Fox lay, George says,
'I told him that it was his purgatory where they had
put me into,' and an Anglican dignitary who justified
the excommunication of Friends for not coming to
Church was told, 'You left us above twenty years
ago, when we were but young lads and lasses, to the
Presbyterians, Independents and Baptists who made
spoil of our goods, and persecuted us because we
would not follow them, and as for the old men
(whom you left behind) that knew your principles, if
you would have kept them alive you should have sent
them your epistles and gospels and homilies and
evening songs . . . and not have fled away from
us. . . . We might have turned Turks and Jews
for any collects or homilies or epistles we had from
you all this while. . . . This is madness to put us
out before we be brought in.' "

"His humour was drawn from a shrewd English
mother-wit which saved him from many extremes. Wish
him extravangances of conduct are dismissed as 'mad
whimseys' and petty criticisms as 'jumbles.' He trusted
his heart rather than his logic, and, had he lived,
would probably have made short work with the rigours
of discipline with respect to dress and behaviour."

CHAPTER II

THE QUEST FOR SIMPLICITY

THE QUAKER GARB FOR MEN AND WOMEN became almost a uniform. It was not however intended as such in the first place. Quakerism started at a time when the different grades of society could be distinguished by the clothes they wore.

Quakers therefore in dress, as in their plain "thee" and "thou," desired to emphasise the unity of all men by adopting the plain dress of the average man and woman of the day. They also regarded the changing fashions as waste and display. The plain costume at the time of their foundation was continued and by accident rather than design became the Quaker garb.

Naturally the young were always seeking to break away from this austerity, whilst older Friends were constantly seeking to uphold it. Many Minutes revealing this are on record. Here are two Minutes stated with such fullness of detail that they might be headed "The Complete Quaker" and "The Complete Quakeress.":—

The Complete Quaker

From Aberdeen Quarterly Meeting in 1698, we have an elaborate Minute directly resulting from a visit of two Irish Friends. It furnishes a complete guide to the approved garb for men and women.

"First, among the men, we condemn all shooting with guns of any sort for game or recreation; all shooting with bows and arrows, all playing at dams (draughts), golf, billiards or any other foolish game so called; and are sorry and ashamed any of our youth should need any caution to such things. Also we condemn all hunting with dogs and hawking, as altogether unsuitable to that weighty testimony God hath called us unto.

"Also in their apparel we condemn:—all broad ribbon for hat bands, all cocking up of the side of their hats, all vain powdering of wigs or their own hair. As also all their bushy and long cravats, fringed or speckled.

We condemn their false shoulder pieces, like necks of shirts, called by several "cheats" and desire they may put comely necks to their coats; We condemn their hand-bands of cuffs like shirt sleeves; We desire that their coats may be buttoned to the top and not some buttons kept loose to make a show with their cravats.

Let all their big cuffs and flapping sleeves be cut off and make meet with the rest of their sleeve. Let all superfluous buttons and blindholes be put away and the buttons further down than needs for fastening their coats. Let the pockets of their coats be in the inside and so needless slits and show of ranges of buttons be prevented on the outer side of their coats; and (let) all needless lips and superfluous cloth be forborne in their coats, and all rows of heads of stockings at their knees be altogether forborne and let plain buckles be in their shoes."

The Complete Quakeress

Having thus adjusted the man's dress from top to toe, Aberdeen Meeting turns to the women, "either younger or elder."

"We jointly do desire: they forbear vain cutting or shedding their hair to set it out in their faces or foreheads; but that it be put straight back; and that they wear on their heads a plain coif, without any ruffling or needless lips in the front of it: and their hood above it, without any wire or paste-board to keep it high; but let it be tied straight or low, and not waving loose about their faces. And let not long laps nor "maseind" laps be on their hoods or head cloths —an ell or an half being judged to be fully sufficient for their hoods about their faces, laps and all.

Let none wear ruffled neckcloths, but either plain bands or plain napkins. Let their mantles or other gowns be made plain, without broad or ruffled tips on the shoulders of them and without lead or great rows on the sleeves of them, but only a plain uplay thereon;"

Advices and Rules of 1811

Some idea of the greater strictness of earlier days may be gathered from the following quainter extracts from *Advices and Rules agreed to by the Yearly Meeting of Friends in Ireland,* published in Dublin in 1811. If these are the quainter extracts, there is much else in the 226 quarto pages which is beautiful and helpful to present-day Friends. To emphasise this it would be well to put down first the concluding advice.

Finally

"Finally, Friends, collectedly and individually, farewell! May all our meetings be held with weight, as in the immediate presence of the heavenly President. May the aged among us be examples of every Christian virtue; and evince, by the calmness of their evening, that their day has been blest. May the middle-aged not faint in their allotted stations; but together with their elder and younger brethren, firmly support, yea exalt, the several testimonies which we are called to maintain. And, O! may the beloved youth, the tender objects of our care and of our hope, bend early and cheerfully under the forming power of truth: that thus, each standing on his allotment, the harmony of the building may be preserved, and we may truly grow up into a holy temple for the Lord."

Play Reading and Novels

"This meeting being sorrowfully affected, under a consideration of the hurtful tendency of reading plays, romances, novels and other pernicious books, it is earnestly recommended to every member of our society, to discourage and suppress the same."

Parliamentary Elections

"It is earnestly recommended that Friends keep out of the agitation and party spirit, too frequently prevalent at elections of members of parliament, whereby the mind is drawn from that quietude and stability in which it ought to stand, and which is so necessary for our safety and preservation."

Few Words, and Savoury (an excellent advice)

"We beseech you, in your ordinary conversation among men let your words be few and savoury."

Music Meetings

"We apprehend some are in the practice of drinking healths, gaming, frequenting playhouses, music meetings, and other places of diversion which practices are inconsistent with the gravity and sobriety required of the professors of christianity."

Cringing and Bowing

"Advised against a declension crept in among us, by unbecoming gestures, in cringing and bowing the body by way of salutation, which ought not to be taught or countenanced."

Thee and Thou

"There being a desire felt in this meeting, that Friends may keep to the plain language of thee and thou to a single person; as also to stile* the days and months, first, second, third, etc.; and not to balk truth's testimony by taking or keeping off the hat either in a customary way, or to shun the cross to any

---

*" 'stile'—the correct spelling of 'style' "—Skeat

person or company, many of our elders having greatly
suffered for bearing their testimony faithfully in those
points.''

Bending the Knee by the Female Sex

''Friends are advised against uncovering the head
in salutation or in courts of justice, etc., and bending
the knee by the female sex; . . . for the
maintaining whereof our ancestors suffered deeply.''

Indecent Warmth

''Advised, that Friends, in meetings of business,
watch over their own spirits; that no indecent warmth
get in, whereby the understanding may be hurried,
and hindered from a regular judgement on the affairs
before the meeting.''

Children to Dispose of in Marriage

''Parents who have children to dispose of in
marriage are tenderly advised not to make it their
first or chief care to obtain for them large portions or
settlements of marriage; but rather be careful that
their children be joined in marriage with persons of
religious inclinations, suitable dispositions, temper,
sobriety of manners and diligence in business
(which are things essentially necessary to a comfortable life).''

Vain Customs and Fashions

''And that neither any of us, nor our posterity
may degenerate from the point and self-denying

example of the primitive christians, and of our faithful predecessors, in this weighty concern of marriage, by going into the vain customs, fashions and extravagant practices, out of which they were redeemed by the truth; we tenderly advise and earnestly entreat all, both old and young, to avoid such things, as also preparations for finery or excess of apparel, unnecessary attendants, giving gloves on such occasions, making large or costly entertainments and inviting unnecessary guests, which tend to cause hurry, and sometime unprofitable discourses, not becoming those who profess to be followers of Jesus Christ."

Marriage not at a Quaker Meeting

"This meeting advises parents whose children marry by a priest, to be cautious not to receive them into favour too soon (which might be some encouragement to others to run into the like evil); but that they and their friends keep a due distance from them, until they manifest a godly sorrow for their disobedience."

Even the Very Young

"There appears great departure from that plainness and simplicity which are consistent with our christian profession; we wish parents to consider their situation—may we not say, their awful situation(!) and closely to examine their own conduct; to consider whether they do not (even some who make a plain appearance themselves) encourage pride and vanity in their children, by dressing them, while very young, in a manner far from true plainness and simplicity."

Superfluous Fashions

"Advised, that Friends take care to keep to truth and plainness in language, habit, deportment and behaviour; that the simplicity of truth in these things may not wear out or be lost in our days, nor in our posterity's. . . ."

O that our Young Women

"To our great grief we find too many of our young men, instead of observing that gospel exhortation to be sober-minded have given way to lightness and vanity; the pernicious effects whereof have led them into pride, and such extravagancies as those who are not of our professions observe, as marks of declension from our primitive plainness. And O that our young women, likewise, would cease from all unseemly and immodest appearance in their apparel!"

Pictures

"In this meeting hath been revived our ancient testimony against superfluous furniture in Friends' houses, such as pictures particularly."

The ban on pictures seems strange now, but even in my childhood the only pictures were engravings.

The White Quakers

This simplicity in dress and furnishing was carried to excess by a break away of some Dublin Friends,

who termed themselves "The White Quakers."
They refused to have any colour in their houses. It is
startling, especially to those who saw in the last war
the gradual disappearance of coloured china, to read
how the wife of the leader of "The White Quakers"
took all her coloured china into the street, and there
smashed every piece. I once heard a Salvation Army
lassie, in similar circumstance, say: "Before I was
converted I had some nice jewellery which I loved
to wear. When my life was changed I knew if I
continued to wear it I should go straight to hell—so
I gave it to my sister!"

The zeal and earnestness with which the Quakers
felt their responsibilities in plain or simple living is
well illustrated by the deep concern which Joseph
Pike and his cousin Samuel Randall felt when nomi-
nated by Munster Province Meeting to visit Friends
on the subject of plainness. They first put away all
superfluities out of their own houses.

Plain Clothes—Plain Houses

Joseph Pike has left an account of this in his
Journal. He says: "it is with me here to mention,
as a memorial to my children and their children's
children, some particulars of the fine and superfluous
things which, for truth's sake, we were willing to
part with; and our dear wives also joined in spirit
with us, by putting away their silk garments, instead
of which, they got plain stuffs. As to our own clothing
we had but little to alter, having both of us been
pretty plain in our garb. But my dear cousin, being

naturally of a very exact and nice fancy, had things in more curious order as regards household furniture than I had, and therefore as a testimony against such superfluities and that spirit which led into it, he not only altered or exchanged (as I did) several articles that were too fine, but even destroyed some of the finest things we had. Our fine veneered and garnished cases of drawers, tables, stands, cabinets, scrutoires, etc., we put away or exchanged for decent plain ones of solid wood without superfluous varnishing or ornamental work, our wainscots or woodwork we had painted of one plain colour, our large mouldings or finishings of panelling, etc., our swelling chimney pieces, curiously twisted bannisters, we took down and replaced with useful plain woodwork, etc., our curtains with valances, drapery and fringes that we thought too fine, we put away or cut off; our large looking glasses with decorated frames we sold or made them into smaller ones.''

A Present-day Conclusion

Isabel Grubb in *Quakers in Ireland* is well worth quoting here:—

"This may amuse us now, but the extracts I have given show under what a deep sense of concern these rules (for plainness) were promulgated and how the Quaker of that time realised that the smallest and most insignificant factor of daily life was not without its bearing on our attitude towards God.''

The Friends carried their principles into their business life, as can be seen from the following story.

Sir Walter Scott and a Quaker

The business of William Sessions Limited has been in Quaker hands from its start. It was founded in 1811 by William Alexander, whose bookshop and printing press can be seen in the Castle Museum at York. In 1814 he added printing, because he was "concerned at the worldliness of the books being published" and founded his press to publish worthy books. They are extremely worthy, even although by modern standards they are also dry!

Walter Scott spent some time in York collecting local colour. During this time he formed a friendship with Alexander, who is said to be the original of Dr. Dryasdust, in the introduction to *The Antiquary*. Wishing to do a good turn to his printer friend, Scott suggested that Alexander should try to secure the printing of *Ivanhoe*. The sturdy Quaker however replied: "Walter Scott, I esteem thy friendship and I value the kindliness of thy suggestion, but I fear thy books are too worldly for me to print." What would William Alexander have said to a modern "crime" novelist?

Red Shoes

We think of our Quakeress ancestors as always clad in sober Quaker costume, with nothing allowed beyond grey. The younger ones were however, seeking ways and means of adding something more attractive, and were reproved for so doing by their

Women's Meeting; sometimes their mothers also being reprimanded! It is, however, a little startling to find a Women's Meeting reproving an erring young sister for wearing red shoes, and even red stockings, under her Quaker grey.

Going to Quarterly Meeting

It was fear of some gay addition to the Quaker costume which made Thirsk Women's Meeting direct that young women intending to go to the Quarterly Meeting should first appear before the Women's Meeting "in those clothes that they intend to have on at York."

Quaker Colours

We think of Quakeresses as dressed in grey or brown, but this was only their desire to keep away from the changing fashions of the day. Thus, when brown and grey were in fashion a Colchester woman Friend, on being shown brown and grey when buying cloth for a cloak, exclaimed: "Take away those gaudy colours; I prefer plain scarlet." "Plain scarlet" is at the present time the everyday wear of the older country women of the West of Ireland. It is thus possible that this Quakeress was wanting to be dressed in the ordinary colour of the countryside.

It was for another reason that Harvey the Scientist once startled a Manchester meeting by appearing in a new suit, perfectly correct in Quaker cut and simplicity, but of a bright red in colour. This was purely accidental, as he was colour blind.

The Quaker men did not escape the attention of their meetings as will be seen from the following:—

Wigs

The Epistle from the Half-year's Meeting, Nov. 1684, states that several Friends "who have hair enough on their heads, do without any real necessity cut it off and get great ruffling periwigs, and others who have some necessity for want of hair or some other infirmity do get such periwigs as are superfluous in length or otherwise."

A later Minute advises Friends who design to cut off their hair and get wigs to consult their Monthly Meeting first!

Long or Short

The typical Quaker costume for men included breeches and stockings. When long trousers came into fashion many men Friends adopted these for their greater convenience, which led to much shaking of heads at thus following fashion.

W. A. Green relates that his great grandmother used to tell of an elderly Quaker who bemoaned this conformity to the prevailing fashion with regard to long trousers, adding, "But praise be to God, there is still a blessed remnant in shorts."

The Planting of Gardens

Even gardens were seriously considered. Wm. C. Braithwaite in his *Second Period of Quakerism* relates: "We find Friends warned against admitting unsuitable persons to business meetings, particularly guzzling drinkers and company-keeping smokers! Proud-like, unsettled girls or lasses are not to accompany travelling women Ministers, and inquiry is to be made what Friends' sons keep 'greyhounds or hunting dogs.' " Friends are reminded in a Minute of rich Irish flavour (Half-year's Meeting, November, 1705) that there may be a great superfluity and too great nicety in gardens. "It is therefore desired that all Friends in planting gardens do it in a lowly mind and keep to plainness and the serviceable part, rather admiring the wonderful hand of Providence in causing such variety of necessary things to grow for the use of man than (seeking) to please a curious mind."

Vain Sports

Naturally sports were not approved, as will be seen from this story.

About 1861, before the authorisation of the "unanswered queries," Westminster Monthly Meeting was considering "Vain Sports or Amusements." One member thought all Friends were clear, another hoped it was so, and a third thought the usual return might be sent in. There was however, in the Meeting one, Thomas Trusted, who was notoriously fond of partridge shooting. The Clerk, Nathaniel Morgan, turned to him with the query: "Any exception, Cousin Thomas?" to receive the reply, "No! 'tain't the season," so all Friends were clear.

Speaking from Notes

Apparently even speaking from notes was not approved by Yearly Meeting. When Josiah Foster was Clerk he turned on a speaker and said, "Thou art speaking from notes! Thou canst not deny it! I heard them rustle."

When Marmalade was New

A little girl about 1850, was sent with some needlework which her mother had done for some Friends.

Marmalade had just then been introduced and it was a great luxury, so when the little girl had delivered the parcel, the lady said to her, "Would thee like a slice of bread and marmalade, my dear?" Being shy she said, "No, thank you," though she longed for it.

When she got home and told her mother, the child said, "I thought they would ask me again, and then I was going to 'Yes.'" Her mother looked at her in surprise and said, "Don't you know they are Quakers? —and expect your 'yea' to be 'yea' and your 'nay,' 'nay.'"

The Quaker and the Fox

The Duke of Grafton was fox-hunting one day, when a Quaker on an eminence pulled off his hat and gave a "Yoicks, tally ho!" The hounds ran to him and so lost the scent. The enraged Duke galloped up to the offender and asked, "Are you a Quaker?" "I am, friend," replied the man. "Well then," rejoined his grace, "as you never pull off your hat to a Christian, I will thank you in future not to do it to a fox."

CHAPTER III

COURTSHIP AND MARRIAGE

THE OLD-TIME FRIEND did not recognise Cupid—he was a heathen god—but his darts penetrated equally effectively both Quaker grey and the gayest fashion. Amongst Friends, however, the steps leading to marriage were most carefully enquired into and considered, as will be seen in this chapter.

A Hint not Taken

A spinster Quakeress of over seventy related how in war time she could get no-one to cut the ivy on her house, so she mounted a ladder and started to cut it herself. A bachelor neighbour passing said: "You want a man for that job." Said she, "I've been wanting a man all my life and never got one." The visitor to whom this was told asked, "And did he help you with the ivy?" Said the Quakeress, with a twinkle, "He did not take the hint either about me or the ivy."

One of the most delightful Quaker love stories is a century or two old, but will be read with pleasure to-day.

Dost thou love me?

"Martha, dost thou love me?" said a young Quaker. "Why Seth," said she, "we are commanded to love one another." "Ay Martha, but dost thee

28

regard me with the feeling the world calleth love?"
"I hardly know what to tell thee, Seth; I have
greatly feared my heart was an erring one. I have
tried to bestow love on all, but I have sometimes
thought that thee wast getting more than thy
share."

The timid lover is of course not confined to any
particular class of people, but here is a Quaker one.

A Shy Suitor

A very shy and bashful young Quaker was staying
with relatives and obviously wanted to propose to
one of them, but could not come to the point.
The visit was near its end, and his futile attempts
were so embarrassing that finally the daughter who
was obviously his choice said to him, "Cousin, is
there something thou very much wants to say to me?"
He admitted that there was. "Then let it be as if it
was said" she told him. They were married a few
months later.

I. and R. Poley in their American *Quaker Anecdotes*
have a somewhat similar story.

Modest Proposal

A very timid Friend was deeply in love with the
daughter of a near-by Quaker family. He went on
loving her for eleven years without proposing.
Meanwhile he built an attractive house with gardens
and out-buildings. When it was all finished he invited
the family of his beloved maiden to come to see his
home. He took them all over it and although the
relatives saw to it that Anna and he were left together,

nothing happened. Finally he took her to see the out-
buildings. As they leaned over, looking into his
empty pig stye, he turned to her affectionately and
said, "Anna, shall we keep a pig?" The quaint
proposal was effective, a pig was bought, and "they
lived happily ever after."

Three other stories from the same book will interest
Friends in this country.

Satisfied Spinster

A Friend of Sandy Spring, Maryland, lived unmarried all her days. When she was quite advanced
in years, someone asked her why she had never
married, to which she replied. "It takes a mighty
good husband to be better than none."

Another Reply

Another Quakeress, also unmarried, replied to a
similar question, "I may have missed the best, but I
have escaped the worst."

What's in a Name?

To the Friends' Hostel at Jordans came very late
one night a young couple, asking for accommodation.
The Warden first reproved them for disturbing the
repose of the household; then remembering her
responsibility for Quaker hospitality, she asked,
"Are you Friends?" To which the young man
replied reassuringly, "Oh, no, we're married."

The above four stories have crossed the Atlantic,
the last one crossing and re-crossing, now here is one
of a Friend crossing himself.

Freedom

A Friend was going to America to be married and this was one of the good wishes he received: "Some men have crossed the Atlantic for freedom, but thou to lose it. I trust it will be all stars and no stripes and thou wilt have as much freedom as thou hast wit to secure."

The last voyage was to America, the following one is of even a longer journey.

Marrying a Quaker

A Quaker, on a voyage to Australia, heard an otherwise charming lady swearing hard on several occasions. When he was in conversation with her one day, he mentioned that, being a Quaker, her swearing distressed him. He was surprised at the answer. "So you're a Quaker too. I am swearing hard, but you see I'm marrying a Quaker, so I'm getting it out of me."

Quaker Weddings

The Quakers refused to go to church to be married but, from their start, took themselves solemnly in marriage in Meetings, held sometimes in Meeting Houses and sometimes at Friends' houses. These weddings were really illegal, but fortunately were early tested in the courts.

In 1661, at Nottingham Assizes, Judge Archer and a jury decided that a particular Friend's marriage was lawful and the child of it a lawful heir. This decision was never afterwards challenged.

It will thus be seen that Quaker marriages were only legal by case law, and it was many years before

Parliament passed an Act making Quaker wedding procedure fully lawful. Because of this difficult legal position, great care was taken to secure the correctness of Quaker registers.

There was even greater care taken that the young Friends did not lightly enter into matrimony. The woman Friend had to appear before the Women's Meeting, the man before the Men's. Then they had both to appear before a joint Meeting.

A Quaker Wedding Certificate

Here is the wording on the Wedding Certificate of William Walpole and Elizabeth Roberts, dated February 9, 1718 (The italics are mine):—

" . . . having declared their intentions of taking each other in marriage *before several public meetings* of the people called Quakers at Mountmellick, Mountrath and Castledermot according to the good order used among them, whose proceedings therein after a *deliberate consideration thereof* were approved by the said meetings, *they appearing clear of all others*, and having consent of parents *and relations* concerned" (notice having been twice further given) and *still nothing appearing to obstruct.*"

The "declaration" varies from our modern one, and is stated to have been "made in a solemn manner." It is: "Friends you are witness this day that I take Elizabeth Roberts to be my wife, promising her through the Lord's assistance to be a loving and faithful Husband until death separate us."

The signatures are interesting as showing how people then spelt their surnames according to their own fancy. The husband and wife sign as "Wallpoole," the Walpole relatives who sign as witnesses sign as :— "Wallpolle," "Wallpoole" (four times), "Walpool" and "Walpole."

The phrase, "having consent of parents and relatives" will be noted. Young people to-day are restive about parental consent; what would they say about securing the consent of their aunts!

No mere Formality

It was no formal appearing before a Meeting. The Minutes of Thirsk Women's Meeting show this. Twenty-one Friends joined in a testimony against a young man who "took his full cousin to wife over the head of the Monthly Meeting." When an intention of marriage was announced it inquired into the young woman's clearness from similar engagements "then left them at liberty to accomplish the said marriage as way may open," and appointed two Friends "to see to the orderly conducting thereof." On one occasion it suggested the marriage should be postponed until the young woman was "clear of another young man Friend."

Saying the Words

The young folks had therefore, to go through an ordeal before their marriage was allowed, and to this day the ceremony itself remains a further ordeal. At a Church wedding the bride and bridegroom have their backs to the congregation and have to say but few words and those carefully given to them to be repeated. At a Quaker wedding the two face the Meeting and, standing alone, repeat their words unaided. I remember the wedding of an engine driver. As I looked at his set face, I said to myself, "That's how he looks when running at speed on a rainy night through a junction, with a maze of points and signal lights." Nor is it an ordeal only for the unaccustomed speaker. James Hogge, afterwards the Member of Parliament for East Edinburgh, was a practised speaker and never more at home then when facing hecklers at a large open-air meeting, with a fine memory for facts to confound the questioner. Yet, when he had to "say his words" at York Meeting he completely broke down. It was only the whispered help of his bride, coupled with a kiss she gave him in front of everyone, that enabled him to struggle through the simple phrasing. It is well the Wedding Certificate adds to its statement of what is said by the couple, "or words to that effect." One bride in York meeting in her nervousness promised to be "a loving and faithful husband."

Marrying Out

Marrying outside Quakerism meant, for long years, being turned out of the Society; indeed my own father, so late as 1873, was the first man in York Meeting to "marry out" without being disowned. The following story well illustrates this fear of parents lest their children "married out."

Princess Victoria

A young attaché of the United States Legation met the Princess Victoria (afterwards Queen Victoria) at a diplomatic reception and had the honour of twenty minutes conversation with her. Naturally, he was delighted with this favour, and wrote home in glowing terms about the Princess and his conversation with her.

His Quaker mother in America, to whom, as to most mothers, no girl was too good for her son, knew nothing of Court etiquette and wrote back saying how interested they had been by his letter, but, "thee know, we should not like thee to marry out."

In the days when "marrying out" meant disownment, it was a real problem for a young Friend living in a small Meeting to meet a helpmate within the Society. Yearly Meeting served a useful purpose in bringing Young Friends together. I remember an Uncle saying, with a chuckle, that his brother had been to Yearly Meeting to "look round."

The difficulty of meeting a suitable helpmate within the Society is also illustrated by the two following stories:—

Married Out

A Quaker had married out, and Friends were duly deputed by his Monthly Meeting to visit him. Their report included the following, by way of excuse: "It should be stated that our Friend was only led to take this step after much exercise within our borders."

A Quaker maiden of sixty became engaged to a

Presbyterian elder. A deputation waited on her about her "marrying out." She replied: "I've been waiting sixty years for the Meeting to marry me. If they did not want me to marry out, why didn't they bring along their men?"

Although divorce is almost unknown in Quaker marriages, doubtless because of the injunctions on the young people to take careful and prayerful thought beforehand, everything did not always run smoothly as the two following stories show. Both are at least a century old.

A Mother-in-Law

In the Minutes of Thirsk Monthly Meeting there was sometimes difficulty in answering the Query about are all Friends "living in love," as the following Minute of 1758 shows:

"This meeting being informed that there is some difference between . . . and his mother-in-law, appoints three Friends to see if they can get things reconciled betwixt them."

Obey—or not Obey

The Quaker form of marriage leaves out the promise of the wife to obey her husband, but one Quakeress declared to a friend: "It is true I did not promise to obey when I was married, but I might as well have done so, for I had to do it."

CHAPTER IV

HUMOUR AT MEETINGS

HUMOROUS STORIES ABOUT QUAKER MEETINGS may
seem at first out of place, yet smiles and laughter are
amongst the very good gifts of God. They should, on
occasion, not be out of place in a Quaker Meeting.
One reason for humorous stories about Quaker
worship arises, however, from the fact that anyone
can get up to speak at the Meeting, so that any crank
or person who likes to hear himself talk can do so.
The wonder is, not that there are stories about Quaker
worship, but that they are so few.

One reason for this is that Elders are appointed to
watch over the ministry of their Meeting. These
encourage Friends whose words are helpful, particularly any who have just started to "speak in
Meeting." The Elders also discourage any whose
addresses are "not to edification," to use the Quaker
phrase.

The Elder Met his Match

This work of discouraging an unhelpful speaker is
carried out with loving tact, but sterner words have
to be used to a crank who disturbs a Meeting. One
such, not a Friend, had to be told flatly that he must
not speak in Meeting. He came however the next
Sunday, and again spoke unhelpfully. He hurried off
as soon as the Meeting had finished, but an Elder

caught him up in the street, and started quietly to admonish him. Whereat the erring speaker said in a loud voice, "I can't hear you. I can't hear you, besides you've been drinking, I can smell your breath." The elder was a Bootham master. He was ahead of his boys, but not by much, and they were hurrying to hear what the shouting was about, so he decided quickly that he would seek a more suitable occasion!

Notices in a Prayer

Rufus Jones was once present at an all-day Meeting. During the closing prayer, the minister remembered he had omitted some of the notices. This is what he said: "Thou knowest, O Lord, that there is plenty of lunch for all who may wish to stay, and Thou knowest, O Lord, that there is hay in the shed behind the Meeting House for all the horses."

The right or wrong choice of even a single word can make such a difference, as is illustrated by these two stories.

The Gadarine Swine

A Friend had just finished a sermon on the Gadarine Swine, when another Friend got up and began with: "We have been listening to the words of the poor demoniac."

An Unusual Beginning

A Friend, at the wedding of his nephew, began his address, "On another melancholy occasion."

A Misprint

A Quaker Meeting decided to hold a meeting open to the public. Unfortunately in the notice the printer dropped one letter from "Society of Friends." It was the letter "r."

The tired and the old sometimes pass from meditation to sleep in a long silence in a Quaker Meeting, which is the point of the next story.

Drowsiness

In 1739, at a meeting at Chester, U.S.A., John Salkeld, jovial and sometimes eccentric, saw several members overcome with drowsiness. He suddenly sprang to his feet and shouted "Fire! Fire!" Everyone was then awake and asking "Where?" He responded, "In hell, to burn up the drowsy and unconcerned."

The well-known pioneer mental hospital at York, The Retreat, has given rise to several stories, in the first of which we can all endeavour to join.

A Pithy Sermon

A patient at The Retreat once gave this short, but pithy sermon, "Dear Friends, let us try to be good."

H. C. Hunt's *A Retired Habitation* has another story of the difficulty the head of The Retreat has in deciding between the benefit to the patient of attending Meeting and the possibility of some words being said more amusing than helpful—there was the woman patient who started with fervour "Oh for a bubbling up, oh for a bubbling up," then her mind refused to work, and she added, "Oh for a bubbling up of raspberry jam" and sat down. Most often, however, the contribution by the patient is helpful to the meeting.

This story out of *A Retired Habitation* is of the beginning of the Nineteenth Century and concerns

Alexander and The Retreat Patient

A Friend patient at The Retreat was allowed to come to Meeting, but it was considered better that he should not speak. A member of the Meeting, William Alexander, the printer, helped in this by sitting behind the patient and drawing his coat tails through the back of the seat. When Alexander thought the patient might rise to speak, the coat tails were pressed firmly against the seat. The patient once outwitted Alexander. After all had risen for prayer he did not sit down, but waited standing until the Meeting had settled down. He then quoted his text, "Alexander, the coppersmith, did me much harm," and sat down.

The next story is of a dear old Friend, who was a minor poet. His great joy was to see his poems in print. If we smile at the story, we can at least see his point of view in being allowed to carry on his ministry, which had been helpful to Friends before his illness.

Funerals

A patient at The Retreat was a Quaker Minister. It was thought better for his illness for him not to speak in Meeting, but the Doctor thought that as funerals took place in The Retreat grounds, the patient might have liberty then, and he often took part very acceptably. Coming away from a funeral he expressed to my mother his appreciation at thus being allowed to take part, in these words: "These funerals are a boon."

The Fire with a Dull Glow

Some years ago, in the course of a Yearly Meeting discussion, William E. Wilson likened the condition of many of our Meetings to a fire burning with a dull glow because the sticks were a bit damp. Then, after a pause, he said, with great emphasis, "What we need is a lot of dry sticks."

Which?

A woman Friend used to repeat a verse of a hymn and then go on in rather a sing-song voice. One of her Meeting remarked he never knew which was hymn and which was her.

The Sword and Mace*

A Friend, Thomas Clayton, was Lord Mayor of York in 1893-94. He desired that the Corporation in their robes should pay a state visit to Clifford Street Meeting. There was some exercise of mind amongst Friends about admitting the state sword and mace, but finally it was decided that they be allowed as they were the symbols of authority and not lethal weapons. Thus on the appointed Sunday, Thomas Clayton, in his fur-edged red robe and golden chain,

*For revision and illustrations of this story, see pages 45-49 More Quaker Laughter.

sat in Meeting with the sword and mace crossed in front of him on their clips.

John Wilhelm Rowntree knelt down to pray and the Meeting rose. A *Daily Graphic* artist (it was before the days of Press photographers) took this opportunity to make a sketch of the scene, which duly appeared in his paper.

A Quaker Meeting in "Punch"

A *Punch* artist (not realising that prayer was taking place) saw the possibilities of the picture, for J. W. Rowntree's head had been drawn just below the business end of the mace. His picture in *Punch*, by very slight alterations, depicted Joseph Spink Gray, in the Ministers' Gallery, bringing down the Mace crack on J. W. Rowntree's head, whilst Fielden Thorp, our grave head of Meeting, chuckled with delight and Maria Richardson and my Mother, Mary Sessions, were depicted smiling in keen enjoyment.

When does Meeting Begin?

Non-Friends are sometimes puzzled as to when a Friends' Meeting starts. Hannah Maria Crosland used to relate how she was once sitting beside a uniformed Salvation Army lassie and overheard her whispered prayer, "Lord stir 'em up, Lord stir 'em up." H.M.C. then whispered to the Salvation Army officer a few words to show how the Meeting was active although silent. This led to understanding and there-fore to a unity with the periods of silence in the Meeting.

A Friends' Meeting versus a Salvation Army Band

A Salvation Army officer told me that he might have become a Quaker. He was impressed by what he had seen of individual Friends and so decided to attend one of their Meetings. When nothing apparently happened, he asked his neighbour, "When does the Meeting begin?" Unwisely the Friend just 'shushed' him up, instead of whispering to him the reasons for the silence. A few minutes later he again put the same question and was again 'shushed.'

Then he heard a Salvation Army band playing from its earlier open-air meeting to its gathering at its 'barracks.' He told me he said to himself "These people don't begin when they start—that lot outside start before they begin." He walked out of the Quaker Meeting and followed the Salvation Army band. Later he joined the Army and became one of their officers.

The Meeting had Begun

When the falling off of attendance at worship began to exercise people's minds, the *Daily News* sent its reporters round to count attendance and to give their opinions of the services. One was sent to a Quaker Meeting. This non-Friend waited wonderingly for the Meeting to begin. Then, as the silence continued, he caught the spirit of worship in the Meeting. His words ran something like this, "I suddenly became aware the Meeting had started; it was only that I was slow to enter into the worship."

The Fur Tippet

If the silent beginning of Meeting puzzles a visitor for the first time, so does the ending. There is silent worship, then suddenly there is a general stir, for Meeting has ended. Closer observation would show that the two Ministers, or the two Elders at the head of Meeting shake hands, to mark the close of the Meeting. In a smaller Meeting where there is only one Minister or Elder, the position is a little difficult.

The little Kirkbymoorside Meeting had no Ministers and only one Elder. It broke up when this Elder, Ann S. Hartas, put on a little fur tippet which she wore for Meeting in summer and winter for this purpose.

Bread or Sandwiches

At one Meeting, Members on Preparative Meeting Sunday brought "packed lunches" with them, so that, after the Meeting for Worship, the business could be transacted without hurry and followed by a congenial social time.

A Member of this Meeting was in a bus with her little boy and was talking to a neighbour, who was a Plymouth Brother. By chance their conversation turned on their respective religions and the neighbour said: "It is true, isn't it, that you do not break bread at your Meetings." At which the little boy joined in with—"but we sometimes bring sandwiches."

The hurry of modern life is largely responsible for the decay of morning or evening Family Worship, which was so valuable, with its few quiet minutes of peaceful thought of higher things before and after the varied activities of the day. There was the reading of a passage from the Bible followed by silent or vocal prayer. Two stories have come to me from this of the reaction of family pets which were present.

The Parrot and Family Worship

A visiting Friend took the opportunity of the morning family worship to make a very long prayer. The old parrot listened in silence for some time, then said: "Turn him off."

Moses the Cat

Early in this century, Edward Grubb was giving a few lectures to Friends in the neighbourhood of Belfast and was staying with a middle-aged couple whose names were Isaac and Rebecca. There was no family except a favourite cat whose name was Moses. It was very intelligent and would answer to its own name. One morning after breakfast Isaac was reading aloud from Exodus: "And Moses said. . . . " A prompt "Miaw!" came from the cat.

The Toll Bar

The last surviving Toll Bar near York was on the way to Huby, where York Friends held a monthly service in the disused Meeting House. Preachers going to preach were exempt from paying toll, and the old toll-keeper had always accepted the statement that the Friends were going to a Quaker Meeting. A new toll-keeper insisted, were they "preachers going to preach?" Being Quakers they did not like to

presume that they would have "liberty" to preach,
yet being Yorkshire Quakers they did not wish to pay
the toll. After some discussion they were passed
through free on my father's formula; "We are going
to hold a Quaker Meeting; it is likely we shall preach,
but if we do not we will tell thee on our return and
pay toll both ways." They preached.

Meetings

The visits of American Friends are very welcome
and helpful, but the visit of two who came over about
fifty years ago was considered not as edifying as those
of other American Friends, as will be seen by this
story of

Taking the Meeting

At Cardiff Meeting the man Friend prayed, his
wife prayed; he spoke, his wife spoke; he again
prayed, he again spoke, his wife again prayed. There
was then about five minutes or so left before the
normal close of Meeting, when he somewhat startled
the little band of worshippers by remarking: "If
anyone has anything to say, they'd best be sharp."
Whether this put anyone off speaking I do not know,
but no one else took part, and with a few added
words of prayer our American Friend concluded the
Meeting.

Late to Meeting

The "gathered silence" with which a Quaker
Meeting commences makes late comers more disturbing than with other modes of worship, when for
example the late comer can enter under cover of a

hymn. The Elders therefore often urge Friends to be all assembled by the time the Meeting is due to begin. This advice was twisted to suit the occasion in the story of a rather fashionable young Friend who came to Meeting ten minutes late and the door keeper would not let her in. She explained that the Book of Discipline advised Friends to "assemble at or near the hour appointed"; whereupon he immediately opened the door.

Bottled up Laughter

Is there any laughter so hearty as when it has had to be hastily checked and some further incident makes it over-run all the desire to check it!

In my young days two or three young Friends were put on the Yorkshire Quarterly Meeting Arrangements Committee, so that the door-keepers knew fully of the Agenda. Our elders were discussing turning the Small Committee Room into a Rest Room, when there seemed other needs for it. John Stephenson Rowntree asked, "Does any Friend use a Rest Room?" Then added, "Except A.C." This good Friend had a reputation for making the most of her ailments, and our elders started to laugh, but hastily stopped, for they realised this laughter was unseemly before the young door-keepers. Unfortunately the next remark made was: "But there are others who like a Rest Room besides A.C."

This mention again of A.C. was too much for the bottled-up laughter of our elders and it exploded. How they laughed; casting guilty glances at the young door-keepers! We youngsters thoroughly enjoyed the incident, and we thought the more of our elders for being so human.

Writing of laughter suddenly checked and then becoming uncontrollable, recalls an incident at Ackworth School.

Potted Missionary

We called corned beef "potted missionary." Thus, when at a British and Foreign Bible Society meeting one speaker introduced another as "a real live missionary" and repeated with extra emphasis "a real live missionary," we began to laugh. Frederick Andrews at once put up a hand to stop us, and we stopped. Unfortunately the speaker started again where he had left off with "a real live missionary." Hastily bottled-up laughter had to have its outlet, and this time wise F.A. let us go on, whilst the speaker stood wondering what in the world he had said to cause such gusts of laughter. Presently F.A. stopped us and rose to tell our visitors about "potted missionary," whereat the speaker, "the real live missionary," and the school laughed again together.

An Exciting Quarterly Meeting

We think of Quaker Business Meetings as quietly and peacefully doing their work, but the early days brought divisions before the new society settled down to its orderly ways. William C. Braithwaite in his *Second Period of Quakerism* gives an account of an exciting Quarterly Meeting.

"In the Wilkinson and Story divisions at the end of the seventeenth century it is recorded that one Curtis, a supporter of Wilkinson and Story, being sole trustee of Reading Meeting, and the party disliking Women's Meetings, refused the premises to the Women's Quarterly Meeting, locking the doors and forcing them to gather in an adjoining malthouse. Curtis declared against women gadding about the country away from their household duties. At the same time, April, 1682, Benjamin Coale, one of the party, was clerk, both to the Quarterly and Monthly Meetings, and, after a disorderly scene was displaced in the former and two Quarterly Meetings resulted, held on the first occasion at the same time and place, but at different ends of the room, each with its own clerk.

Less exciting but more amusing is the case of the mistaken identity of a twin.

I am Samuel Henry

Samuel Henry and Moses James Adams were twins, who, even when grey-headed, kept remarkably alike. Samuel Henry Adams had attended a Quaker Conference with Fielden Thorp. Fielden Thorp duly gave his report to Monthly Meeting and regretted the absence of Samuel Henry Adams; he added, "I notice however that Moses James is present and, as doubtless his brother will have told him some of his impressions of the Conference, perhaps he can add to what I have said." Dutifully accepting the invitation, 'Moses James' rose with the words, "Please! I am Samuel Henry."

Hello! Twins Again

Which reminds me of a Printers' Conference at which one of the Doig twins of Newcastle was present, who, although over 60 years of age, had kept remarkably alike. Doig was walking down the hotel corridor when he said "Strange! my brother's come after all; we agreed I should come, whilst he would look after the business." Walking down to greet his brother and ask him why he had changed his mind, Doig found there was a big mirror at the end of the corridor and he was looking at his own reflection! This is the only case I have come across of a twin mistaking himself for his brother.

Here to end the chapter are a few short stories.

A Family Report of a Business Meeting

"A.B. put the Committee's report very clearly, but it only seemed to make woolly-minded C.D. put his foot down more firmly in the clouds!"

New Duty of the H.S.C.

During a morning session of the Home Service Committee the following telegram was received: "Home Service Committee prevented burst pipes."

Joan of Arc and the Bible

At York Friends' Sunday School, a teacher, introduced Joan of Arc into the lesson. A Bootham Master was therefore amused to be told by his small son that Joan of Arc was a character out of the Bible, as he had learnt of her at Sunday School.

Canon Atkinson in *Forty Years in a Moorland Parish* related this story of

A Quaker Funeral

The mourners stood solemnly round the grave for over half-an-hour with never a word spoken, until a leading elder turned to the sexton with the remark: "Our Friend seems vara comfortable. Thou mun hap him oop."

An Unusual Grace

At a Breakfast Meeting for unemployed men, held at a Quaker settlement, one of the workers inadvertently gave vocal thanks "for the messy blessings we have received."

Quaker Grace

The Cadburys invited a party of Friends over their works and then took them out to lunch. In the midst of the silence of Quaker grace, one of the waiters was heard to say to another, "Don't these blokes have grace?" To which the other replied, " 'ush, they're a-'aving of it now!"

Dr. Johnson on Women Preaching

Boswell recounted to Dr. Johnson his visit to a Quaker Meeting where he had heard a woman preach. Dr. Johnson ungallantly remarked, "Sir, a woman's preaching is like a dog walking on its hind legs; it is not done well, but you are surprised to find it done at all." Friends, whose Meetings are often much helped by vocal service from their women members, will entirely disagree with Dr. Johnson's opinion.

CHAPTER V

QUAKER SHREWDNESS

THE QUAKERS HAVE A REPUTATION for shrewdness. It has even been said they make philanthropy pay! This last remark is probably founded on the success of well-known organizations, such as the Quaker chocolate firms. The fact is that these firms were founded out of a desire to use the raw materials of the West Indies and thus find employment for the freed slaves, whose economic position was very bad immediately after receiving their freedom. The founders at the time thought of this venture as a side line, which is shown by the fact that Joseph Rowntree, the elder, put his youngest son in charge of the new cocoa factory, whilst he and his older sons continued in the family grocery business.

Fixed Prices

The relative prosperity of Friends was also the result of their desire for their yea to be yea and their nay, nay. The Quaker shopkeeper sold at a fixed price, plainly marked. This is accepted to-day as the soundest business method, but at a time when shopping meant keen bargaining, the Quakers at first lost custom through asking what they regarded as a fair price, and sticking to it. It was not long, however, before the advantage of this brought more than the lost trade back. The child could be sent to the Quaker's shop to buy at as good a price as the keenest bargainer. The young wife, freshly come to the district, found it safer to go to a Quaker shop, where she bought at as good a price as her mother-in-law, who was so much more experienced in bargaining! Hence, sound business methods, founded on religious principles, brought increasing prosperity to these early Quaker business men.

Living quietly, dressing plainly, using well-made but simple furniture, also brought an economic reward. The early Quaker's household and personal expenses were low in comparison with his more ostentatious neighbour. He thus saved more for prudent investment. This point is well illustrated by the story of:

A Footman behind her Carriage

Nicholas Wain was a wealthy Friend, yet kept his simplicity of mind. His wife thought otherwise and considered it would be suitable to have a footman behind her carriage. The wish being so frequently expressed, her husband at last promised to comply with it. The next time the carriage was ordered for the purpose of making a stylish call, she was gratified to see a footman mounted, although surprised that he did not get down to open the carriage door for her. However, when she arrived at her place of destination, the door of the carriage was opened in very obsequious manner by the new servant; and great was her surprise and confusion to recognise in him her own husband.

There was also a desire to avoid waste, which is well illustrated in a story given in I. and R. Poley's *Quaker Anecdotes*.

Habits of a Lifetime

An elderly Quaker lady, rich in this world's goods, fainted one day. As she was being given a whiff of aromatic spirits of ammonia, she opened one eye and said, "Don't waste it. Put the stopper in the bottle."

There are many stories about Thomas Firth, one of which has been given in the chapter on 'Humour.' Here is one he enjoyed telling against himself.

A Quit Payment

Thomas Firth, of Lane Head, near Huddersfield, had a man who came yearly to make a small payment for rent. Thomas Firth one year asked him if he would like some refreshment, and the man replied: "I dean't (don't) mind if I do." T.F. said, "If thou doesn't mind, I don't," and let the man go at that. The next year the same question received a decided acceptance. An uncut cheese was brought. "Wheer mun I cut it, Mr. Firth?" asked the man. "Thou may'st cut it where thou likes," was the reply. "Then, if you've no objections, I'll cut it at whoam," said the man and proceeded to carry off the cheese, much to Thomas Firth's amusement at the way in which the man got his own back, and that a year afterwards.

A Vast Change

There is a book *The Friends, what they are, and what they have done*. A Quaker bookseller was astonished by this very slight change in wording when asked by a customer for "The Friends, what they are, and who they have done."

There is unconscious humour in

Slime for Friend Josiah

Dr. Thomas Hodgkin was a celebrated London physician (uncle of the well-known historian of the same name). He was fond of telling how, when driving to call on a patient, he had found a Friend in a muddy pond into which the latter had been thrown from his horse. "It was black, thou knows, it was very black. It was as if all the sweeps in London had been there to wash. He was covered with black slime. I took him into my carriage; *but I could not take him to my own house*, so I took him to Josiah Forster's."

Spectacles or Eyeglasses

General William Booth, the founder of the Salvation Army, told Ethel M. Sessions he regretted that Quakers had left off the plain costume and were following the fashion and frivolity of the world. The uniform prevented this in the Salvation Army. She, being in her late teens stood up to him with, "Tell me then why your Salvation Army lasses wear eye-glasses instead of spectacles?" Surprised, the General asked why they did? to which my sister replied, "Because eye-glasses suit the Army bonnet so much better." General Booth pondered this in silence.

The present generation will hardly know what "eye-glasses" are, although they were much in use thirty and more years ago. They were twin glasses held together by a spring which clipped on the nose and having no arms reaching round the ears.

This is an old story, but it is a story with a lesson.

Where dids't thou feel?

A gentleman was relating to a Quaker a tale of distress, adding, "I could not but feel for him." "But did'st thou feel in the right place? Did'st thou feel in thy pocket?"

Whisky and Soap

A Quaker called Fowler kept a Temperance Hotel. Commercial men liked it, but they did not like the temperance side and were always bribing the maids to bring to their rooms something stronger than the house provided. One evening Friend Fowler saw a maid on the stairs who said she was taking up some hot water for shaving. As this is usually needed in the morning Fowler was suspicious; he smelt it and said, "Thee had better let me soften it to make a better lather" and proceeded to mix soap with the traveller's whisky and hot water.

The next story comes from Ireland from the fine collection Ernest H. Bennis has made.

The Placing of a Comma

Paul Abbott of North Abbey, Youghal, was an importer of goods from the Continent, at a time when privateering was common. One time his ship was boarded by these pirates. Nothing daunted, he explained he was Paul, Abbott of North Abbey, Youghal, Ireland, whereupon they thought it better to leave such a holy man alone.

This reminds me of a Mount School girl with a good brain, but a total incapacity to spell. Her essays at Oxford were much enjoyed by her tutors, the matter was so good, the spelling so very bad. On her landing card on a visit to the continent whilst still at college she filled up the line "Occupation" with "Nun," and was surprised how much more quickly and easily she was passed through the customs than her companions.

Taking Offence

Joseph Firth Clark was a welcome visitor at the Yorkshire Adult School Co-operative Holiday. Walking down the street from the train he was espied by some Adult Scholars who had arrived earlier. One joyously called across the street: "Why here's t'od lad, and there's t'od lass too!" Someone said to J.F.C. afterwards, "You and your wife (a stately lady) are not often addressed in that way, but you did not seem to mind." He quietly said, "I have learnt in the course of a long life never to take offence when no offence is intended."

It should be stated that "t 'od lad" means in the Yorkshire Dialect "the old fellow." "Lad" and "lass" are used for people of any age. I once stopped at a Yorkshire woollen mill to ask the way, and was told there was a lad who was going there and would show me if I gave him a lift. The speaker added, "He won't be long, he's just drawing his pension." The "lad" turned out to be nearly eighty and glad of the lift.

Cleaning the Factory Window

The Bench were considering a rather trivial case under the Factory Act and dismissed it. The Factory Inspector asked for "a case to be stated," adding unwisely, "perhaps your Worships may not know the law on this point." Magistrates often do not know the law, their learned Clerk is there to keep them right on this, but they do not like to be told so. One magistrate showed his annoyance at this remark; the other, a shrewd Quaker grocer, looked bland and childlike as he prepared to listen to the Inspector. Those who knew "Treacle Tommy," his popular nickname, knew trouble was coming for the Inspector, and presently it came. "Now thou said if the boy was cleaning the factory, say cleaning the factory windows, he would be employed in the factory." "Certainly," said the Inspector, delighted to have made his point. "Now" said Treacle Tommy, "if the boy was cleaning the outside of the factory windows would he be employed in the factory?" In the laughter, which greeted this sally, the Inspector muttered something about not teaching the magistrates the law, which was just what he was doing, and abruptly sat down.

Here is a delightful story of

The Matter of a Subscription

A rich Quaker, generous to local charities, was diffidently asked for a subscription towards rebuilding the parish church. The Friend hesitated, but learning that the project included pulling down the old church, he asked how much this part of the scheme would cost. After more thought he finally said: "Thee was right in supposing my principles would not allow me to assist in building a church. But for pulling down a church thee may'st put me down for a hundred pounds."

The defence might well have used the following story in the case of the Portuguese fraudulent bank notes, which went through all the courts to the House of Lords on the question whether the Portuguese Treasury lost the face value of the unlawful notes, or only the cost of printing them. In each court there was only a majority of one judge who held that the loss was the very much higher face value, and this story would seem to show that the judges in the minority were right.

Money to Burn

I do not know if the phrase "money to burn" is founded on this instance of one of the Quaker Backhouse bankers of Darlington, who, staying the night at an Inn, met a miner who had come into some money and, having celebrated the event too freely, offered the Friend to throw sovereigns with him into the river. This was naturally refused. The miner became abusive, so to quieten him the banker produced some notes of his own bank and said he would burn notes with the miner. The man at first demurred, as he had no notes, but the banker offered to exchange the golden sovereigns of the miner for the notes. This being done the two, to the gasping astonishment of the others in the room, burned note for note until the miner had had enough. The miner was in reality burning his golden sovereigns, the banker only the cost of printing some more notes.

The story usually ends there, but one version, and I think the true one is that the Quaker sought out the miner the next morning and found him sober and sorry. The sovereigns were returned, less the cost of printing the notes. I like that typical touch of Quaker shrewdness—and fairness—in, "less the cost of printing the notes!" for it was in the days when bankers issued their own notes.

From a Barclay Bank advertisement there is another banker's story.

Bringing Home the Money

A Barclay, one of the Quaker bankers, was driving along a turnpike road in a post-chaise with a heavy load of money. One of the front wheels came off, and could not be put back. Nothing daunted the Barclay-in-charge piled all his bags of money and himself over the opposite rear wheel and the postillion was thus able to bring the load of money safely to the bank.

It is curious that I have another and more circumstantial story of a similar incident, given by a descendant of Jonathan Backhouse, Amy E. Wallis. It is quite possible that the Barclay of the story remembered what the Backhouse had done, or vice versa; or else that some teller of the story has remembered the point of the story but put it down to another banker. I will not cast doubt however on either story, but tell them both.

The Broken Wheel

Early in the nineteenth century some dispute arose between Lord Darlington of Raby Castle, and Jonathan Backhouse, the Quaker banker. The former gave notice to his tenants that they were to pay their rents in Backhouse's notes, intending to allow them to accumulate until he had collected a greater number than the banker could—on sudden demand—pay in gold.

This project of the nobleman became known to Jonathan Backhouse, who immediately posted to London, obtained a large supply of bullion, with which he hastened back to Darlington. When passing through Croft, one of the fore wheels came off the chaise, and could not be replaced. To wait for a new wheel would make him too late, so the banker piled the gold at the back of the chaise, and by carefully "balancing the cash," was able to reach Darlington on three wheels.

By this feat the bank was so well provided with specie that when Lord Darlington's agent presented a very large parcel of notes, they were all promptly cashed, the Quaker quietly remarking, "Now, tell thy master that if he will sell Raby Castle, I will pay for it with the same metal."

For long the incident of the wheel coming off upon Croft Bridge was looked upon as traditional, but an inspection of the books for 1819 shows the following entries:—

"1819 6mo. 25th. To Bank and Cash to London £32,000" and on 31st of 7th mo. Profit and Loss

Account is debited with "£2.3.0 wheel demolished." These entries lead one to believe that the incidents did occur and that the surplus cash was returned to London. A ballad was published later, with drawings of the incident.

Grown in the Telling

The Darlington story of the broken wheel has evidently grown in the telling. I received another and very picturesque story of the wheel coming off at a lonely place thirty miles from home, just as dawn was breaking. It was the rear wheel. The bags of gold were packed over the other rear wheel (!) and Jonathan Backhouse sat on top of his gold, balancing the chaise on the rutty roads.

In the meanwhile preparations had been made for the run on the bank. A sack of corn and bushel measures were obtained, room being made for some of these in the windows. The others were screwed to the counter. When the gold arrived these bushel measures were partly filled with corn, then golden sovereigns were put on top. The Lord of Raby having advised his poorer neighbours to get their money out, the early comers saw gold everywhere. They were even asked if they had ever lifted a bushel of sovereigns, and tried their strength on the well screwed down measures. Outside they showed their gold, told of the bushels of gold too heavy to lift and that there was more gold than they had ever seen. The run on the bank had thus slackened by the time the Lord of Raby appeared—for in this story it was the Lord himself, with two footmen carrying two huge portmanteaux of notes who came, not his agent. An old cashier, getting slow, and going slower for the occasion, gravely counted the Lord's notes, and as gravely and slowly counted out the gold in exchange.

This story makes the Lord of Raby grow weary of this long proceeding, and seeing gold appearing readily in exchange for his notes, and bushel measures of gold still untouched, he gave in and paid both the gold and the remaining notes into the bank. Then follows the remark about buying Raby Castle.

All I need say in considering the two stories is that the man who told the last one was an excellent story teller and the additions he put in would doubtless have satisfied Dr. John Watson's dictum, "provided the addition be good."

The next story is interesting, because it is unfinished and we are left to finish it ourselves.

Who Gives Way?

In a very narrow lane close to Grayrigg Meeting House, near Kendal, a Quaker and the Squire met in their respective traps, where there was no passing room. The Squire said that, as he was the owner of the land, the Quaker must back out. The Quaker declined, saying he had so much further to back out, and so had entered the lane first. After glaring at the Quaker for some minutes, the squire pulled out a newspaper and began reading it. He soon tired of this and, with an impatient gesture, was just about to put it in his pocket when the Quaker mildly said, "Friend, if thou hast finished reading thy paper, wilt thou kindly lend it to me?"

And here to end the chapter are a few short ones.

The Quaker and the Organ

"Friend Maltby, I am pleased thou hast got such a fine new organ in thy church." "But," said the Clergyman, "I thought you were strongly opposed to having an organ in a place of worship." "So I am" said the Quaker, "but if thou wilt worship the Lord by machinery, I would like thee to have a first-rate instrument."

The Public Revenue

In a Yorkshire Meeting when the Query had been read asking Friends whether they were careful to avoid defrauding the public revenue, an old Friend arose and said, "In reference to the Query which has just been read, I wish to advise Friends to take very good care that the public revenue does not defraud them."

The Way to York

A traveller, lost on a Yorkshire moor, met a Quaker and said to him, "This is the way to York, is it not?" To which the other replied, "Friend, first thou tellest me a lie and then thou asketh me a question."

A Pickpocket

A Friend to a pickpocket, caught in the act of stealing his watch, "Nay, friend, nay, I cannot spare thee the time".

CHAPTER VI

HISTORY: GRAVE AND GAY

THE EARLY FRIENDS travelled far in the Service of Truth and had concern to speak with the rulers of the lands they visited. Perhaps the most remarkable story of these travels is that of Mary Fisher:

The Quaker "Witch" and the Sultan

Mary Fisher visited America about 1660 in the Service of Truth where she was accused of being a witch, but "having no spot of her which was insensible to pain when pricked with a pin," she was saved from the stake and sent back to England.

Here she felt she had a message to the Sultan of Turkey. After great difficulty, and after being turned back twice, she eventually came to the camp of the Sultan. She was given an audience, delivered her message to the Sultan, and returned safely to England.

Suffering in America

The first part of the above story illustrates the strangest part of the persecution of the early Quakers, that in New England by the Puritans, who had themselves left England to escape from religious persecution.

This New England persecution was very bitter, as will be seen from the account of how Mary Clark suffered in 1656 in Boston:—

New England Persecution

Mary Clark "came thither under a religious concern to warn those persecutors to desist from their iniquity. She delivered her message to merciless men, who rewarded her with twenty stripes of a three-corded whip, and detained her in prison for about twelve weeks in the winter season. The cords of these whips were usually as thick as a man's little finger, and the stock sometimes so long that the hangman made use of both his hands to strike harder."

A typical example of these visits to Kings and the heads of States is that of Thomas Shillitoe.

A Concern for Rulers

He secured an interview with George III. He presented to the Prince Regent, afterwards George IV, a religious address, in which he plainly set forth the Prince Regent's sins and wildness. He interviewed the Prime Minister of Denmark, and so secured an audience with the King. The Prime Minister told Thomas Shillitoe that his clothes were hardly suitable for an audience with the King, but the Quaker replied simply that they were the only ones he had. He saw the King of Prussia. He also interviewed the Czar of Russia. To all these rulers he talked plainly of the evils existing in their lands.

Another great Quaker traveller, William Allen, talked with Kings, and his fearlessness is shown by this incident:

Sugar and Slave Labour

William Allen was invited by the Emperor Alexander of Russia to take tea with him. William Allen found the tea sweetened, and politely told the Emperor that he could not take it because sugar was the product of slave labour. The Emperor recognised the sincerity of the refusal and at once ordered a cup of unsweetened tea.

Sugar in Pies

Until the freeing in 1833 of the slaves in the West Indies, then the only source of sugar, it was an almost universal custom of Quakers to do without sugar in their tea; although, as Joshua Rowntree observed in later life, "I do not remember that this prevented sugar being put into fruit pies." Evidently the desire was to cut down the use of sugar, not to do entirely without it.

The visits of William Allen had an interesting result.

An Emperor at Meeting

In 1814 the Emperor of Russia and the King of Prussia were in London and were visited by William Allen. Expressing a desire to attend a Quaker Meeting, the Emperor, together with the Empress, two Dukes and the Russian Ambassador, attended, the last in full regimentals. The Empress duly sat on the women's side of the Meeting House with a Grand Duchess in attendance.

Elizabeth Fry was directly responsible for the strangest meeting of all.

A King in Prison

The King of Prussia, on a visit to England in 1842, was interested in the prison work of Elizabeth Fry, and went on one of her prison visits with her, attended by some nobles, and the civic dignitaries of the City of London.

Of the simple service which took place, *The Times* related: "The scene at this moment [when Elizabeth Fry was praying] was indeed a strange one—at one view the beholder witnessed the Monarch of a great nation—a portion of the nobles of the realm—the wealth and authorities of the great Metropolis of the commercial kingdom, approaching with prayer their common Creator, in unison with those whose vice and crime had made them occupants of a prison!"

Friends travelling in the "Service of Truth" as they termed it, were not only wishful to visit Kings, for there was an historic Meeting held in the United States.

A President at Meeting

Joseph John Gurney had a concern to hold a Meeting in Washington with the officers of government, and the members of Congress. He was granted the use of the Legislation Hall. The President, and other officers of the government, and many members of the Congress and their ladies attended. The Meeting followed the silent worship of Friends, and Joseph J. Gurney spoke.

It has already been noted that Thomas Shillitoe addressed the Prince Regent on his wildness. Perhaps it was this introduction to Quakerism which led the Prince Regent into the following escapade:

The Prince Regent as a Quakeress

George IV, when Prince Regent, dressed himself as a Quakeress, and attempted to penetrate the mysteries of a Women's Meeting. Although his Quakeress costume was perfect, his boots and his unfeminine posture aroused the suspicions of one of the women Friends present. Going out she summoned two men Friends, who tapped the Prince on the shoulder and led him quietly out.

It is more probable that the Prince Regent's interest in the costume of a Quakeress and in a Meeting of Women Friends may have come, not from Thomas Shillitoe, but from the following incident:

The Prince Regent and a Quakeress

Mary Lidbetter, in the cautious words of the *Friends' Quarterly Examiner*, was "unusually good looking." She was of such beauty that she attracted the attention of the Prince Regent in 1797, as she was walking through the streets of Brighton, dressed in Quaker garb. The Prince swore she was a woman worth looking at, even although she had an ugly bonnet. He followed her, and in a narrow place, barred her way, and demanded a kiss. Mary Lidbetter, with an arm strong with the farm churning, answered him with such a stinging slap on the face, that he was utterly taken aback, and did not trouble her further.

Quakerism in Pennsylvania

So long as Pennsylvania was ruled by Quakers with a policy of unarmed fair-dealing with the Indians, there was peace. Even when Friends lost control, and wars broke out, the Quakers pursued their peaceful methods.

War Paint at Meeting

The picture of Indians in war-paint at a Quaker Meeting is a correct record. Some Indians on the war-path surrounded an American Meeting House, intending to slaughter all inside. A scout found the door open, and looking through saw the Friends, unafraid, engaged in silent worship. He and his fellow warriors came in, piled their arms in a corner, and sat quietly through the Meeting, then silently went their way.

It was not only at Meeting, but in the isolation of their settlers' cabins that Friends upheld their belief in the protection of peace.

The Unlocked Door

In the Indian wars the settlers withdrew into forts, often the scene of fierce fighting and the massacre of the inhabitants. The Friends, strong in their peaceful intentions, hid their hunting pieces and other firearms, and left their doors unbolted. The Indian scouts of parties on the war-path would lift the latch, and, if the door was unbolted, the war party would pass on.

A further American story is a fine illustration of the devastating effect of a quiet retort.

The Erie Canal

When the building of the Erie Canal to connect the Great Lakes with the sea was being discussed there was much opposition, including that of the Quakers on religious grounds. A Friend summed up this religious objection by saying: "If God had intended

Lake Erie to be connected with the sea, He would have done it originally." There seemed to be no argument to refute this until an elderly Friend rose and quietly quoting: "And Jacob digged a well," sat down again.

Whilst mentioning America it may be interesting to add that a Friend, Joseph Hewes*, was one of the fifty-six signatories of the Declaration of American Independence and that Herbert Hoover, a former President of the United States, is a Quaker. There are, and have been, many Friends in the British Parliament, of which the best known was John Bright, famous for his speeches on behalf of the repeal of the Corn Laws.

John Bright's Speeches

John Bright was an orator whose speeches were understood by everyone. He used to rehearse them to his gardener, who stopped him if he did not understand any part. John Bright said that if a passage was not clear to his gardener then it would not be clear to his audience.

Possibly John Bright's most famous passage was when speaking on the Crimean War—"the angel of death is abroad in the land; you can almost hear the beating of his wings."

Frederick Andrews in a lecture on elocution, advising on the wise choice of words, quoted this passage, paused, and said, "Now let me change but one word, and all the beauty has gone,—'You can almost hear the flapping of his wings.' "

*But see More Quaker Laughter, p. 67.

To Lose the Hat or the Head

A deputation of Quaker and other nonconformists was waiting in an ante-room to present an address to the Prince Regent. The Friends kept their heads covered. Before the deputation was received, footmen came along and took off the hats of the Quakers. Dr. Waugh, a Wesleyan, said, smiling, to the foremost Friend, "Persecution, brother," to which the Friend replied, pointing to the portrait of Charles I, "Not so bad to take off the hat, as the head."

Mention has been made of some historical Friends' Meetings, and there was one such more recently.

An Eastern Quaker Meeting

When the British Cabinet Mission went out to India to try to settle the Indian question on the spot, there were two or three interesting Quaker Meetings. Each of them was attended by members of the British Cabinet Mission, by prominent Indian Nationals, including the sister of Pandit Nehru, and by leading Moslems, including Sir Hassan Suhrawardy. Mahatma Gandhi attended the second.

Mr. Gandhi, at his evening prayers, spoke highly of the calm atmosphere which prevailed there. "I greatly admire the silent prayers," he said, "We must devote part of our time to such prayers. They afford peace of mind." He also said: "Emptying the mind of all conscious processes of thought and filling it with the spirit of God unmanifest brings one ineffable peace, and attunes the soul with the Infinite."

Friends were surprised after the 1939-45 war to find how high up Quakers were in Hitler's list of

Societies to be suppressed when England was invaded. Possibly the following views of Quakerism widely held in Germany, particularly that of the secret society, may have been the reason.

A German Idea of Quakers

Before the 1914-18 war a number of Mary Owen's German pupils were given an essay on "Comparative Religion." One wrote: "The Quakers are very good people. They spend nearly all their time in doing good works. They dance in their religious services. They are a secret society. No one can join the Quakers— they must be born Quakers. The Quakers are never allowed to marry."

Mary Owen adds: "My pupils came from various parts of Germany—Prussia, Bavaria, the Rhineland, Baden, etc.—but they all held in common the belief: (a) The Quakers are a secret society; (b) The Quakers dance at their religious services; (c) That one is born into Quakerism, and can never join the Society, and (d) That marriage is forbidden in the Society! !"

They told me they had learned these views at School and they were quite convinced the statements were correct. No amount of explanation would shake them.

It is possible to see from which old Quaker customs some of these mistaken ideas have come, and although the idea of dancing at religious services is the antithesis of a Friends' Meeting, it is evident that the confusion has sprung from the name of Quaker.

Coupled with this is an English schoolboy's version:

George Fox, by a Schoolboy

An English boy, preparing for Matriculation, wrote this in an essay on Religious Leaders of England:

The Leader of the Quakers was George Fox. They believed that all warfare was a sin, and they wanted to make other people think so too. So they did not speak about it at all, but they would not fight. They tried to lead good lives, and believed they could influence people by their example, and that silence was better than speaking.

Much might be written on the Quaker days of persecution but Besse's *Book of Sufferings* has really covered all that is to be said, though the reasons for this persecution may be stated.

Quaker Sufferings

The Conventicle Act of 1664, repealed in 1689, made it an offence for more than four people to meet together. This resulted in a Quaker Meeting of five or more Friends becoming an illegal assembly, but Friends decided to continue their Meetings in spite of this Act.

Quakers also refused to pay Tithes. This was defiance of the law. It also gave the parish priest, often already bitter against Friends on religious grounds, a legal hold over them.

The greatest single cause of Quaker imprisonment was however their refusal to take an oath. A hostile bench of magistrates, finding in the Friend no just cause for fine or prison sentence would tender the Oath of Allegiance to the Crown. This, being an oath, would be refused, although a statement of loyalty would be made. This statement would be ignored by the Bench, who would condemm the Friend to prison, as a disloyal person, until he took the Oath. Even when the magistrates were not unfriendly, a hostile accuser, when he saw he was losing his case, would demand that the Oath of Allegiance be tendered, thus putting the Bench in a difficulty if they did not do so. There were cases too when friendly magistrates dismissed the Quaker by tendering him the Oath of Allegiance, only to find they were in a worse difficulty with him than before. In these ways, thousands of Friends were kept in prison for two years or more, for there was no way out. Often the only way of release was by a petition to the Assize Judges.

There were other minor causes which led Quakers into conflict with the magistrates. They would seat themselves in the Court without removing their hats, thus giving cause for any Justice Shallow to start hearing their case with a bias against them. Friends also would give no surety for their future good conduct, arguing that they had done no wrong, even when the letter of the law was against them. They would too, on the same argument, refuse to give surety to appear at a higher court, Quarter Sessions or Assize.

Thus from one or other of these causes the Quakers were put in prison in such large numbers that there were more Friends in prison at the height of the persecution than there were members of the Society at the end of the nineteenth century.

Besse's Sufferings

There is a curious note running through Besse's accounts of the Sufferings of Quakers, in which he records disasters to some of those who assisted in the persecutions, *e.g.*, horses dying after they had hauled away goods distrained from Friends, or an incident such as the following: "It was observed that the Steward of the Court, who was the cause of the fining and had sold the distressed goods, sat down to drink with the Man and his Wife who had bought them, and rising to go forth, fell down, and was taken speechless, and within three days died." Besse adds: "When such disasters coincide with Acts of Persecution, they seem to minister just cause for Reflection among Considerate Persons."

Return when asked

After the first few years of persecution the gaolers began to know the peaceableness of the Quakers and often let them go home on their promise to return to prison when asked. On one occasion the Sheriff having given one leave to go home, issued a decree of escape against him. More often this partial release meant that they were not called up again. More than once a prisoner, given temporary liberty by order of the clergyman by whose means he had been committed to gaol, was by the Sheriff's orders not received back into prison when he returned to give himself up. Some, though really at liberty, remained technically prisoners until their deaths.

Cleared by a Post Mark

In 1722, there was great rumour of an invasion of Ireland by the Pretender and two informers stated that George Bewley and Thomas Beale (Quakers), were assisting this cause and had met for this purpose at a certain house in Cork, one of their meetings being fixed at a certain day and hour. This was serious, as many people had been executed for this offence, including some innocent people who had been falsely sworn against. Fortunately George Bewley found from a letter he had sent to his wife that on the stated day he was, with his old father, visiting a Meeting fifty miles away. The letter moreover had a clearly dated postmark. (Note this was before the days of envelopes, when letters were fastened with a wafer or seal, hence the letter itself and not an envelope bore the postmark.)

The Loss of a Minute

In all, the losses of the Irish Quakers during the war between William III and James II amounted to £100,000. Amongst other subscriptions Friends in the Barbados sent £100. In the Minute Book of the National Meeting is a minute ordering a letter of thanks to be sent to the Barbados. A terse marginal note records "Done, but a French privateer took it." The next letter of thanks arrived safely.

Telescope or Lewis Gun

Joseph Bennis was an ardent astronomer. During the guerilla warfare in 1921, when bullets were flying and houses being burnt down, he placed his telescope out of his house in George Street, Limerick, to view some planet. Very soon there was a thundering at the hall door and a demand to know what that Lewis Gun was doing at the window. The Quaker offered to show the "Black and Tans" the planet he was studying, but they took no interest in planets, and told him that if he did not take it in at once, the house would be burned down.

The Irish Famine

These Irish stories are a reminder of the great work done by Irish Quakers in the famine years of 1845-48, years during which it is computed that about one million people lost their lives through famine, and through the cholera and fever which resulted from the famine.

Irish Friends organized relief Committees and devoted their time and energy to coping with this awful calamity, and to organizing the distribution of food, clothes and seeds. English and American Friends sent liberal supplies of food and clothing. Some came over to help in the distribution, among others William E. Forster, afterwards Chief Secretary for Ireland.

It is interesting to note in connection with the Famine Relief work that all correspondence, whether addressed to Lords or Ladies, to Parish Priests or ordinary civilians began with the old Quaker phrase —"Respected Friend".

Joseph F. Bennis used to tell that, when in a remote part of Kerry, about 50 years after the famine, he happened to mention to an old man that he was a

Quaker. Whereupon the old man began to cry and almost put his arms round him, explaining that during the "black years" he and some of his relatives had been saved from death by starvation by the Quakers.

Extracts from The York Quaker Calendar of 1902

Jan.	1st.	Quarterly Meeting Boys' School opened in Lawrence Street, 1829. (This became Bootham School).
Jan.	13th.	Death of George Fox, 1691.
Mar.	21st.	Quarterly Meeting Girls' School opened in Castlegate, 1831. (This became The Mount School).
Mar.	28th.	John Bright died, 1889.
May	11th.	The Retreat opened, 1796.
May	27th.	Beware—York Races.
July	3rd.	Dedication Service on completion of York Minster, 1472.
July	30th.	William Penn died, 1718, aged 73.
Aug.	26th.	Beware—York Races.
Sept.	1st.	George Fox released from Scarborough Castle, 1666.
Oct.	7th.	John Woolman died at York, 1772, aged 52.
Oct.	14th.	Samuel Tuke died, 1857, aged 73.
Oct.	18th.	Ackworth School opened, 1779.
Dec.	6th.	William Tuke died, 1822, aged 90.
Dec.	23rd.	George Fox reproved Priest Bowles in Minster, 1651.

CHAPTER VII

ODDITIES

It is difficult to classify stories, but most of the following seem to come clearly under oddities.

A writer of to-day chooses a short title, but those of the seventeenth century liked their titles to cover all the ground; here is one:

What's in a Name?

A Quaker, who was suffering in prison "in the Service of Truth" wrote a book entitled *A Sigh for the Sinners in Zion, coming from a Hole in the Wall, by an Earthen Vessel, Known among Men as Samuel Fish*.

Isabel Grubb in *Quakers in Ireland* has a much longer one.

A Title more Pungent than Brief

Anthony Sharp, in the year following the war in Ireland between James II and William III had to defend himself against a charge of being too friendly to King James' followers. He issued a paper which he entitled:

"An Answer to a Libel entitled, 'The White Vizard plucked from the Quakers' Black Faces by way of dialogue betwixt Dick and Thom', the Epistle to the Reader signed J.B. in which his Envy, Falsehood, Profaneness are represented, rebuked, detected and J.B. is proved the Black-faced False Accuser of the said People because He could not obtain his Corrupt Ends of them, by One that desires that Truth may be exalted above Deceit, and that the Innocent may not be condemned and the Guilty go free."

Another of Isabel Grubb's stories concerns

A Public Debate

A public debate on theology took place at 10 a.m. on September 19th, 1722, in the Baptists' Meeting House, Skinner's Alley, Dublin, between Oswell Edwards, Baptist and John Stoddart, Quaker, each having one assistant, the Quaker's being Joseph Gill.

The end seems to have been exciting for the room was so thronged that the galleries began to fall. The reporter ends with the words: "Mr. Edwards having as before proposed the Breaking up of the Assembly and the noise increasing and the Table where I sat and seats about me Breaking, I was for these Reasons prevented from taking the rest of Mr. Joseph Gill's Discourse, who continued his speech for some time longer".

Writing of Irish stories naturally leads to dipping into Ernest H. Bennis' large but unpublished store:

Unruffled Temper

Thomas Grubb (1809-61), a Limerick Friend, had a tailor's shop in George Street, right opposite the County Club. He had the reputation of being possessed of the most unruffled temper. One day his temper was the subject of discussion at lunch at the County Club and one gentleman made a bet with another that he would succeed in causing Thomas Grubb to lose his temper. Accordingly on a busy day, when the Quaker had already been delayed from getting his dinner, this gentleman walked in and asked to see some cloth. Very genially Thomas Grubb took down a roll, but no it would not do. Roll after roll was exhibited and looked over again and again, still without pleasing the customer. At last the gentleman decided on one and asked Thomas Grubb to cut off as much as would fit a penny! This he did, wrapped it up and with a smile handed it to the purchaser, saying, "Thank thee, friend, and the next time thee calls, I hope thy order will be for a larger amount." So the gentleman lost his bet and Thomas Grubb enhanced his reputation.

15 Teamen

Two young English Friends, John and Lodge Scarr, after serving their time to the tea business in London, came to Limerick and in 1850 opened a shop at 15 Patrick Street. Being young and enterprising they placed their name first on the sign over the shop window, then the number of the shop and then their trade. This to the public read as: "Scarr Bros. 15 Teamen from London", and thinking so many men must be able to give good value, customers flocked into their establishment.

A Family Row

Alfred Davis was appointed on the Committee to look after the graveyards of Limerick Meeting. As he had never been to the old one in Pump Lane, his fellow Committee men took him one Sunday after Meeting to view the property. Arriving there, they saw a small crowd, the cause of which Alfred Davis discovered to be a man lying on his back, with an Amazon kneeling on his chest and pounding him for all she was worth. Horrified, Alfred Davis pushed forward and remonstrated, when a voice from the prostrate man said, "If you don't allow us to settle our family affairs in our own way, I'll change places with you". The Quaker did not accept the offer.

Bathing

Miss Betty McC. of G., Co. Cork, was not a Friend. She was very tenacious of her rights; indeed she was known to wander about her land with a large horse pistol in her hand, in search of trespassers. She heard that some of the neighbours, amongst them being W.A., the Quaker, were in the habit of bathing early in the morning in the river that passed through her grounds. This annoyed her much, and finding that notices threatening prosecution were posted up in vain, she told her gardener she would not keep him unless he put a stop to these dreadful practices. Having turned the matter over in his mind, he thought the most effectual way would be to conceal himself, watch for the bathers, and take away their clothes.

One morning as Betty and her niece were sitting in their bow-window at their early breakfast, a tall and portly figure, devoid of clothing, passed the window and rang violently at the hall door, which was quickly opened by her maid, but still more quickly shut. Whereupon W.A. put his mouth to the key-hole and called out, "Tell Betty McC. that brother A., having done nothing to be ashamed of, has come to ask for his clothes."

Betty took out a summons against him for trespass, he against her for larceny of his clothes. Much amusement was expected in Court but neither case ever came on, as a compromise was effected, through the good offices of Friends.

Tithes

A rector called on a Limerick Quaker, who was a barber, demanding 17/6d. tithes. "But I never was in thy church", answered the barber. "That is your own loss", said the rector, "for the door is always open for you to enter".

Shortly after, the rector was surprised to get a bill for 17/6d. from the barber, and called for an explanation, saying he had never been in the barber's place for a hair-cut, shave or any purchase. The barber answered, "That is thy own loss, as my door is open for thee to enter at any time."

Robert Davis has a fund of stories, which are scattered through these pages, but here are two of his:—

Old for their Years

In the summer of 1924, a conference of about 300 Friends, including many from America, was held at Kendal to celebrate the tercentenary of George Fox's birth. On the Sunday evening, at the close of a large public meeting addressed by Dr. Rendel Harris, with John William Graham in the Chair, someone overheard a man asking, "Which of them two blokes was George Fox?"

A Bookshop Notice

Some years ago, when the headquarters of the Society in England was at Devonshire House, I entered the book-shop adjoining the main entrance and, to my surprise and amusement, saw a large card displayed which read as follows:—

TWO BOOKS BY JOHN WILLIAM GRAHAM

THE FAITH OF A QUAKER
Greatly reduced

THE QUAKER MINISTRY
Limp

A local newspaper furnished the following:—

The Medical Lecture

Jonathan Hutchinson, the celebrated surgeon and dermatologist, of an old Yorkshire Quaker family, was apprenticed to Dr. Caleb Williams, a Friend and a Minister. The Surgeon studied at the York Medical School which was very small. Once he was the only student and unfortunately went to sleep. He was roused by the exclamation of the lecturer, "You can wake up now, Hutchinson, I have finished."

The Quaker "Nay"

It is a very old story, that of the child going out to a party and being told to be polite and only to take a piece of cake when she had been asked twice. Alas! the party was given by a Quakeress of the old school and she accepted the child's "nay" as nay, and did not ask her again, so the child had no cake.—Here is a strange version of this:

Pre-natal Influence

During the war we were living in a little village, and were called upon by the local preacher. He asked me to what church we belonged. On hearing we were Friends, he told the following story:—

My Mother used to have dealings with the Quakers, way down in Bristol. They had revivalist meetings, all churches coming together and the best service of all was at the Friends' Meeting House.

The Friends are a real genuine body of people and sincere. Their "Yea" is yea and their "Nay" is nay, there is no humming and ha-ing with them, I've often heard my Mother speak of them. One day, she called upon some Quakers friends about arrangements for the revival meeting and they were just sitting down to a meal of fish. "Will you join us?" they asked. "No, thank you", said my Mother hoping to be pressed, but they never asked her again. They just all sat down and got on with it, and my Mother had to sit there and watch them. As she sat, a terrible craving for some of the fish came over her, but no one thought of asking her again and she naturally didn't like to suggest it. The craving got worse and worse, for she was expecting her first-born baby. When the baby was born, he had the mark of a fish on him. I know that, because this baby is my very own brother, and I have often seen the mark on him, and heard the story. Even now, although my brother is over eighty, as the time for his birthday approaches he is seized with a great hankering after fish, and has to have it served to him.

I put this story up to a medical man. His opinion was that the mark of the fish could only be pure coincidence, but the hankering after fish could be prenatal influence. A similar story, with no mention of the Quaker "Nay," and concerning a lobster, was published in *The Wonderful Magazine*, in 1797.

Then let us have a story from a Quaker pedigree— I believe about an eight-times-great Uncle of mine! It was headed. . . .

Poor Uncle Henry

"Henry H.—was convinced of Truth, walked amongst Friends for several years, ran out, went to the priest for a wife, afterwards he would needs be a shop-keeper. Truth, or the profession of it, gave him credit. He ran into debt, went and built a house with other men's money, and so more and more into liberty until he became a disciple of one called a Conjuror. Turned to keep an alehouse, was arrested and cast into gaol, but his brother redeemed him; his condition is now very miserable, being quite gone from Truth."

This extract from *A Retired Habitation* can certainly be classed under 'Oddities'.

The Roll of Carpet

Long years ago a carriage drove up to The Retreat, the driver reporting that he had brought a patient. The Superintendent went out to receive the new-

comer, but only saw a long roll of carpet. Perceiving
however, a night cap, he had the carpet brought out;
then, taking from it some long wooden skewers, he
had the carpet unrolled. Inside was what the Superintendent described as a "nice little body, who said
those who sent her were as bad as she was."

Writing of The Retreat, may I include a personal
impression of a visit there on Christmas Day?

Too Happy for the Christmas Party

Depression forms part of some mental illness, but
there is also elation. Patients can be happy to the nth
degree, far happier than they could possibly be in
mental health.

In my Christmas Day wandering round, a Male
Nurse suggested I should see 'Mr. X' as he was too
elated to go to the Christmas Day party, and indeed
had had to be shut in his room. I went in to see him
and the door was closed. I tried to keep quiet, but
really he was so merry that he got through my guard
to my sense of humour, and before I knew, we were
laughing together like schoolboys. When I came out
I apologised to the male nurse and hoped I had not
increased his elation. The male nurse thought not,
and said that if next day, he was disappointed at not
being at the Christmas Party, they could cheer him
up by saying he had had a special visit from the
Treasurer.—I wish my readers, some of whom may
think of Mental Hospitals as places of sadness and
gloom, could have been with me and seen the fine
Christmas spirit abroad in the wards and could have
appreciated with me the great work of those cheery,

but tired, sisters and nurses carrying on their mission of healing the sick mind by making difficult people happy on Christmas day.

May I add another personal story, indeed a narrow escape, in a different sphere of activity.

Taking the Salute

In the war the York City Football Ground had been lent for an important Services' match. During the half-time interval, the A.T.S. had given a marching display and after the match I was introduced to the A.T.S. Commander. Said she in a determined voice, "If I had known you were the Chairman of York City I'd have marched you out to take the salute." I said "What would a Quaker do, taking the salute?" Said she, with a still more determined voice, "If I had known you were Chairman, and a Quaker, I'd have marched you out under guard to take the salute!" I replied, "I'm very glad then we were introduced after the match and not before it."

Another wartime story concerns

Lieut. Col. Elizabeth Fox Howard

In 1946, Elizabeth Fox Howard had been acting as hostess of the Quaker Rest Home at Bad Pyrmont, in Occupied Germany. She was rather surprised at having to travel back as a "Lieutenant-Colonel."

Here is a story which illustrates the value of Friends always carrying the wording of the affirmation.

The Grand Jury

The Grand Jury had been sworn and the Judge had begun his address to them when he was annoyed to notice some confusion. A young Quaker had not been sworn and wished to affirm. The Judge said to the equally young Marshal, "Tender him the affirmation and let the rest of the Jury sit down." The Marshal searched in vain in his case for the correct wording, the Judge got more testy, saying "Don't you know it?" The Marshal did not. Hopefully the Judge tried the Quaker, but he did not know it either. Then the Judge said to the Marshal, "I shall have to give it you myself." This he proceeded to do, but in too long bits for two very flustered young men. So after some confused attempts, the affirmation was given about five words at a time, by the Judge to the Marshal, who repeated them to the Quaker, who managed to say them correctly to the Court.

It is a great gift, not sufficiently exercised, to be able to draw out difficult or shy people and make them feel at ease.

Drain Pipes

It was a young Friends' tramp and a local Friend had invited us to an evening meal to meet some members of the Meeting. Amongst these was a newly-joined Friend, whom we were privately informed was difficult to draw out. He certainly was difficult until we touched on drain pipes. To all of us I think drain pipes were but drain pipes; but listening to this man who made them we became quite fascinated.

In the 1914-18 war when conscription came in, it became necessary to appoint Quaker Prison Chaplains to visit young Friends in prison because of their conscientious objection to undertaking military service; hence the following story.

A new reason for joining the Friends

The late Roy Calvert was a Quaker Chaplain at Wormwood Scrubs prison. The majority of the prisoners used to be put down as Roman Catholics, and the Priest was slightly nettled that no prisoners in for crime were classified as Quakers. At last he one day waylaid Roy Calvert at the entrance and with the greatest glee told him that at last there was a Quaker serving a sentence for a crime. Roy rushed to the cell, introduced himself and asked to what Meeting the prisoner belonged. The man said "None" and further "that he had never been to a Meeting." Roy asked "Then why are you down as a Quaker?" The man replied, "Well! I heard they were nice people and thought I would like to belong—just while I am in quod."

Spoonerisms are many, but here is an unusual one:

Henley Friends

At a Monthly Meeting, repairs at Henley Meeting House were under consideration. The Clerk asked for the views of the Friendly Hens.

Burial Grounds

Here are three amusing stories on the unlikely subject of Burial Grounds:

In the course of a discussion in a Lancashire Monthly Meeting on the subject of burial grounds, one elderly man Friend arose and said, "For my part, I wish Friends would make more use of their burial grounds."

The Crowded Graveyard

A narrow-minded Friend objected to the acceptance by Monthly Meeting of an application for Membership because there was no room in the Graveyard.

The Vicar on Quakers

At a Parish Council meeting in Cheshire a few years ago, a discussion took place on the question of the burial of nonconformists. At one point a member asked, "What are we to do with the Quakers?" Whereupon the Vicar replied, "It will give me the greatest pleasure to bury any of the Quakers, any day."

To end the chapter here are a few short stories.

Baptism by Degrees

It was a native, a recent convert to Christianity, who summed up the difference between the religions he knew thus: "The Baptists are big-wash people, the Church of England are little-wash people, the Quakers are no-wash people."

Caution in Speech

A woman Friend, replying to the enquiry "How art thou," said with even more than usual Quaker caution in speech, "Thank thee, I think I may say that I am much as I sometimes am."

A Common Fool

A Scottish Quaker was giving evidence in Court and referred to "First month." Counsel rounded on him and said "First Month! Why can't you give its proper name?" Retorted the Quaker, "Well, if I had said 'Fifth month' I could understand thy difficulty, but he must be more than a common fool who doth not know which is the first month." Counsel appealed to the Judge, "My lud, witness is calling me a fool." "No," replied the Judge, "he said you must be more than a common fool."

The Quaker Arms

A group of Young Friends were rambling in Buckinghamshire and making their way to Jordans. At Gerrards Cross, a few miles from their destination, they called at the local inn for tea. The innkeeper was interested in their movements and on hearing they were going to spend the night at Jordans, exclaimed, "Oh don't go there, the place is full of Quakers." The Young Friends wanted to find out why he did not like Jordans, so they encouraged him to talk, whereupon he told them that when Jordans Village was being planned, he offered to build a Public House, but Friends wouldn't have it. "And," he added, "I did offer to call it the Quaker Arms."

CHAPTER VIII

CHILDREN AND SCHOOLS

I HAD THOUGHT TO INCLUDE a chapter on School
Stories, with sub-headings for each of our Quaker
Schools. Alas, very few have been sent. At first this
seemed strange, for at any gathering of Old Scholars,
stories are told, capped and re-capped, with laughter
and merriment until the small hours of the morning.
Further reflection made me realise that these stories
usually begin, "You remember X". Memory floods
back, and the amusement is partly in the remembrance
of X and only partly in the story itself. Thus when the
stories are written down, they do not seem to be so
funny, and seem hardly so at all for those who did
not know the master or boy of years ago, about
which the story is told. Because of this, children and
schools are together only sufficient for one chapter.

Children's remarks can be very devastating, but
their frankness can also be helpful, as is well brought
out in the story of

The New Elder

Noticing a Friend sitting facing the Meeting instead of in her accustomed place, a little girl asked
her mother, in a by-no-means inaudible voice, "Did
they make her sit there because she wriggles so
much?" Many years later, the now elderly Friend told
the now-grown-up young woman that her childhood
remark had been a lesson to the spiritual pride she
had felt on her first appointment to the Elders' bench.

Stopping Places

It is a common difficulty with inexperienced speakers to have said what was in their minds to say, and not be able to stop. They go on, sometimes indeed repeating themselves, seeking to find a suitable ending. This is trying to any gathering, Quaker or otherwise, and often spoils the effect of what has been first said.

This is well illustrated in the story of a school boy who was rather restless during a long sermon in Meeting. On being reproved afterwards by his mother he excused himself by saying of the Minister, "Well! he did miss several good stopping places."

Questions of Children

The questions of small children in Meeting can be disconcerting. Friends listening to a sermon preached at much length rather united with a tiny girl's audible enquiry of her mother, "Will he be much longer?" We can understand too the young boy at his first Meeting. He had been strictly charged not to talk. The first preacher was his Grandmother. He could be heard asking his Mother, "Why is Grannie allowed to talk, when I am not?"

Here is another child's query.

A Bachus

James Backhouse of York, travelling abroad for several years in search of botanical specimens, returned with a beard, then an unusual appendage. On one of his frequent ministerial visits to outlying meetings,

being short of stature and the partition of the Ministers
Gallery high, only his head appeared above it when he
knelt to pray, indeed when he leaned forward, his
beard hung over it. A small boy was puzzled by this
appearance and the twice-repeated, awe-struck question, "Mother, what is it?" was met in Yorkshire
dialect by "Thee 'ush! it's Back'us." A further
audible question came from the small boy, "Mother,
has Back'uses got tails?"

Another child story comes to us from Ireland.

The Burst Pudding

A woman Friend, an Elder, lived with her grand-
daughter in Cecil Street, Limerick, right opposite the
Friends' Meeting House.

Having to go to the Meeting she left a pudding she
was boiling in a pot in charge of her grand-daughter,
with strict instructions not to let it burst. The pudding
boiled and burst, whereupon the child ran across the
street to the Meeting House and opened the door.
Right in front, in the high-up, old-fashioned Elders'
Gallery, was the grand-mother, who tried by signs to
direct the child to go home, but in a shrill treble
voice the girl called out "It's no use blinking and
winking, the pudding's burst in the pot!"

A story from an unexpected source about a Quaker
Meeting is given in the Memoir chapter of *The
Ingoldsby Legends*.

A Cheeky Boy

The only practical joke in which R. H. Barham
(Thomas Ingoldsby) was ever personally engaged was

when as a boy at Canterbury with a companion he entered a Quakers' Meeting House. Looking round at the grave assembly, the latter held up a penny tart and said solemnly, "Who ever speaks first shall have this tart." "Go thy way," commanded a drab-coloured gentleman, "Go thy way and—" "The pie's yours, Sir" exclaimed the other boy, placing it before the astonished speaker and hastily effecting his escape.

We are but Dust

In a very strict Quaker family of the early nineteenth century an elder sister had been moralizing to her young sister—quite a child—on the transitory nature of all human affairs. This child cogitated on these matters and presently appealed to a good-hearted elderly Friend thus, "Lydia says we are but dust." She received the somewhat matter-of-fact, but reassuring reply, "Tut, thou's made of flesh and blood like anybody else."

Ringing the Bells

It makes our grave and reverend elders more human if we hear how lively they were in their younger days.

James Henry Barber of Sheffield, a very worthy Friend, used to tell, with real enjoyment, how, as a mischievous school-boy, he was sent to conduct a party of young Friends in Quaker dress from another city. On the way J. H. Barber amused himself by ringing door bells. Running to the end of the street, he watched his companions, then only passing by, getting the blame from the irate maidservants.

Family Relationship

A schoolboy wrote in an essay: "The Quakers were invented in the Middle Ages by Oliver Cromwell. They are a very quiet people and never answer back. My Father is a Quaker, but my Mother is not."

Mixed relationships are also present in

The Family Donkey

A Friend "in good standing amongst us," had a donkey on which he used to take out his two little girls. A business acquaintance met him so doing and asked him, "Are these your young family?" The Quaker had a slight stammer, but got out, "Y-yes, t-two of them are, t-the other I p-purchased."

Musical Terms

It was a Mount School girl who declared mournfully that it was no good her going in for a music examination when she didn't know the difference between a crochet and a quaker.

In the next story, although we may think the third freedom rather pagan, we shall at times have very much united with the fourth.

The Four Freedoms

It was a Quaker schoolgirl who described the Four Freedoms of the Atlantic charter as:- "Freedom from want, freedom from fear, freedom from religion, and freedom from speech."

Isabel Grubb in her *Social Conditions in Ireland*, has two interesting stories of schools.

No Burnham Scale Then

In the girls' county school of Charleville, Ireland, the teacher, a local Friend, was given two pence a week for each child; her total salary was about 2/- or 2/6d. weekly.

In Waterford, the schoolmistress was paid 3/- a quarter for each child and it was decided that she "is to get more if she can get Betty Collender to wash the maids" (*i.e.*, the children not the servants!).

The next makes us wonder if the Six-weeks Meeting could not have given its Clerk six shillings for a quarter's course in "writing English."

Scollers Sculling Latin

In December, 1710, the following minute was passed at the Co. Tipperary Six-weeks Meeting, held at Knockgrafton:

"It is ordered by this meeting that all such friends as have sons abrod att Scull doe bring them home and send them too our scull at Clonmel. Samuel Cooke advises this meeting that he hath agreed with William Dover tew keep scull in this county with in the limits of this meeting and to instruct friend's children as a scull master for which he is to have £20 for one year sallary he finding himself diatt lodging etc. Scollers sculling Latin at 9/- per quarter, sifering (arithmetic), and writing English at 6/- per quarter."

In *Quakers in Ireland* Isabel Grubb gives two further pictures of early Friends Schools.

School Fees in 1785

The "bill of admittance" to Mountmellick Quaker School, Ireland, for one year cost £5 and 5/- per week was to be paid for any child who remained at school after the expiration of the time for which the fee had been paid. This "bill of admission" entitled the holder to schooling, diet, washing, lodging and clothing. It was, however, stipulated that the child should bring strong clothing fit to last for four years, and pieces of material for patching! Washing gowns and waistcoats were not allowed.

Quaker Schoolchildren

School books with pictures were not allowed and a Quaker Latin Grammar was issued to avoid the moral unsuitability of the examples and extracts in the current Grammar. Alterations were similarly made for Quaker children in the famous Lilly's Grammar. The learning of French was considered to corrupt the minds of youth and was not to be done without leave from the elders.

Ernest H. Bennis gives a wonderful description of early Quaker education. Special note should be taken of a very Irish touch, where the Irish delight in a fight has overcome the censorship of Quaker Peace principles:—"Throwing stones at his lawful enemies," to wit boys on their way to another school!

Quaker Education in Limerick

In Limerick for Friends' children, about 1800, there was first the non-Quaker Dame's School, run on the same utilitarian lines as that of the immortal Mr. Squeers. The dame taught her scholars to catch rats and mice and practically nothing more. The dunce's cap was in use here, presumably for lack of prowess in the chase.

Having exhausted the resources of this 'Academy,' the boys next went on to a remarkable school kept by a worthy Quaker—one John Tyrrell Baylee. He was popularly known as 'John Tirrible Baylee,' for his pacific philosophy did not run to the extent of withholding corporal punishment, and his cane, 'Tickles,' was held in great awe.

Legends crowded thickly round 'Tirrible' Baylee's exploits with his dreaded cane. Before ever 'The Mikado' immortalized the principle, he was a believer in making the punishment fit the crime.

A certain boy went to the races one day, instead of school. "Where wast thee yesterday, James?" asked John 'Tirrible' next day, as the culprit slunk in ."Plaze sor, I went to the horse races," "And would thee like to go to the horse races again?" Thereupon the unhappy boy was mounted on a lusty pupil's back and soundly whipped round the schoolroom by the pious Quaker, to the tune of "I'll teach thee to go to the races, James." James however, laughed last, for, having a pin handy, he stuck it deep into his unlucky steed's arm, who promptly dropped him with a piercing howl, amid the plaudits of the class.

Charles, another pupil, throwing stones at his lawful enemies, on his way to school, had the misfortune to knock off an old gentleman's night-cap as he stood shaving at his bedroom window. In great wrath the injured gentleman pursued Charles to the school, thirsting for his blood. John 'Tirrible' only shook his head sorrowfully and merely remarked, "Charles, Charles,! I wish thee was as good at thy lessons as at knocking off old gentlemen's night-caps." In spite of this unwonted calm, it is evident that John 'Tirrible' was something of a ferocious pacifist!

Crossing to England, it may be interesting to record the claim of

The First Quaker School

Stramongate School, Kendal, claims to be the first boarding and day school established by Friends. It was started by the local members of the Society some 250 years ago. One of its headmasters was the father of Professor A. S. Eddington, the astronomer. About 1781 a youth of 15 years put all his worldly goods on his back, and providing himself with a new umbrella, he walked the 44 miles from Carlisle to Kendal to become an assistant master at this school, He continued there until, with his brother Jonathan, he became joint headmaster. This was John Dalton, whose promulgation of the Atomic Theory brought an ordered conception to the haphazard experiments of his day.

York Mystery Plays

There was an amusing side-light to these Festival Plays of 1951. In the Last Judgment scene a Bootham master, who had taken the part of the High Priest, was chased nightly through the Jaws of Hell by three

Bootham boys dressed as Imps of the Nether Regions. We had no such luck in my school days!

I make no comparison between the staffs of these twin schools at York; I simply place on record the fact that, in this scene, whilst the Bootham master was chased into the Jaws of Hell each evening, a Mount School mistress, also in the play, climbed the long, winding stairway into Heaven!

Here is another Bootham story

Bogged in the higher Academic World

The new headmaster of Bootham found two well dressed young fellows in the hall, so he took them round the School. They pulled up at the Middle Senior Schoolroom, saying with affection that they had left Bootham from there. "And do you know," said one, "if you examine the records of those who left from the Middle Senior, you will find they did better than the other fellows who left higher up and who've been bogged in the higher academic world!"

The unique place which Neave Brayshaw held in the life of Bootham, and in the affection of its scholars, is well illustrated in this story which the boys loved to tell.

Puddles

Neave Brayshaw died and went to heaven. At the gates Peter could not find his name in the book and so asked, as Neave was sadly turning away, if he had any other name. "Well," said Neave, "the laddies call me 'Puddles.'" "Puddles!," said Peter, "come in at once, we've been expecting you."

By Coach to School

The days when children went by coach to school were times of no holidays. They left their homes only to return after three or four years, grown almost out of their parents' recognition. Here is a story of such children on their way.

A Quakeress was escorting some children by coach to Ackworth School. The Guard was asked at an Inn who he had inside the coach. He replied, "Noon, just rag, tag and bobtail." The Quakeress heard this but said nothing until the end of the journey when she gave him a tip of three coins, saying, "This is from Rag, this from Tag, and this from Bobtail!"

Frederick Andrews

There are many stories about Frederick Andrews, a great headmaster of Ackworth. Years afterwards I learnt he had told the staff at a meal, with one of his famous chuckles, that when I had translated aloud some Latin, let us say, with more originality than accuracy, he had remarked, "William Sessions! William Sessions! I fear thou wilt never be more than Petty Sessions."

Nor shall I ever forget one rebuke of his. We were translating about those in the nether world who were condemned for ever to continue to do the wrong things they had done in life. Looking round for an illustration F. A. remarked, "William Sessions, for example, would continue for eternity to roll that pencil up and down his desk." Doubtless I trifled afterwards in school time, but I never again rolled a pencil!

Poised

The Literature class was a minute or two late in finishing and other classes had started football on the green. Benjamin W. was looking out of the window watching them. We had come to the passage in Tennyson when the damsel poised for flight, stopped to listen to the young knight, "Now," said F.A., looking round for an inattentive boy, "What does 'poised' mean in this passage, Benjamin W." The boy came hastily to attention and said "To kick the football high, sir."

F.A. on Applause

F.A. stopped us at once if we started applause with our feet. He would stand up, hold up his hand for immediate silence and say, "I like you to applaud with all your hearts, but not with all your soles."

Applause at Ackworth School

A University Extension Lecturer called Parkin came to Ackworth School to give a course on Domestic Hygiene. It was a good course, but given in a manner we scholars found dry. In fact we christened the lecturer, "Old dry Parkin" (parkin is a Yorkshire species of gingerbread).

Before his last lecture, word went round to give " 'Old dry Parkin' a good-riddance clap." After the boy and girl mover and seconder of the vote of thanks had nobly said what they could, the good-riddance clap was given with much heartiness. Only

a junior master was in charge. Thus the good-riddance
clap waxed more and more in heartiness, and the
more the lecturer beamed, the more we clapped.

I was sitting opposite to F.A. at dinner next day,
and he asked me, "Sessions, why did you applaud Mr.
Parkin so heartily yesterday? He told his Pontefract
audience last night that he had never received such
warm-hearted applause in his life and he had been
deeply touched by it. I thought you found him rather
dry." "So we did, sir," I replied. "It was a good-
riddance clap." F. A.'s chuckle rang so loudly through
the Dining Room that everyone stopped talking.

One final story of Frederick Andrews.

Amusing thee Sen

F.A. was travelling with a miner and they both
enjoyed their conversation. The miner brought out
his flask and offered F.A. a drink, which was court-
eously declined. "Naa, naa, doo; it's a droop o' right
good brandy" said the miner, but F.A. again said
"no" and told him the reason. "Weel thin, 'ave a
cigar, it's a good yan!" said the miner. F.A. had to
say he didn't smoke. "Does'ta sweer?" asked the
miner. F.A. said "I try not to swear, in fact I don't
think I do." The miner ruminated on this for a bit,
then said, "Tha doesna drink, tha doesna smooke,
tha doesna swear—wot iver does'ta do tive amuse
thee'sen, loike?"

RANDOM GLEANINGS

I come now to various stories worth relating, which do not seem to fit into any of the previous chapter headings. I give them therefore just as they come, without any special order.

A Low Diet

I wonder if this story is as funny as I think it—or do I consider it so because I had to listen to it without a smile, as it was told to me as a tale of woe and illness.

B. Seebohm Rowntree published a chart showing the lowest diet upon which a family of five could exist in fair health. This was the cause of the following story:—

I met a big, burly Adult School man who had been ill and asked him how he was. He replied "I's gettin better now, but me and t'doctor, and 'appen (perhaps) Maister Seebohm, had a bit of a mix up, which put me back quite a lot. Doctor said I 'ad tiv (to) go on a low diet. "Waht's yon?" I said. Doctor told me loike (like), an' I said, "Maister Seebohm's got out a chart on which you can just exist, would that be sort o' low diet?" Doctor said it would be fine, an' I were to come in a month's toime. I did'nt half loike this 'ere low diet, bein' a 'earty eater, but, howsumever, t'Missus said I'd better try it, an' I did. But 'twere no good, niver a bit o' good at all.

"At t'month's end I goes tiv t'Doctor an' I says tiv 'im, "Doctor, this 'ere low diet's na good. I's na better, an' I's fatter than I were." "Then you haven't been sticking to the diet," says t'Doctor. "But I 'as," said I. " 'Ave you t'chart?" says t'Doctor. I 'ad and I lets 'im 'ave it. 'E runs 'is finger down it an 'e says "You can't get fat on this" an he tells me I must 'ave been eatin' in between meals, but I tells 'im I 'adn't. So 'e axes wot I 'ad for breakfast an' I tells 'im, whilst 'e ran 'is finger down t'chart. Then 'e fair beals (roars) out, "Man alive you've been eating the rations of the whole family of five!" "Noa," says I, "niver!" for I were astonished, loike. Doctor asked me about some of t'other meals, then he said I 'ad eaten t'lot. I says, "I wonder if you're reight, doctor, for sometimes when I wearn't feelin peckish loike, t'last mouthful or twa took a bit o' gettin' down, even tho I'm a 'earty eater".

"Weel upshot of it were doctor divided up Maister Seebohm's chart for yan (one) only. My word it were low diet too. Maister Seebohm calls it existence, it were fair starvation for me, but it got mi fat down an' I's feelin' better now."

"Maister Seebohm" comes into another story:

A Question of Relationship

John Wilhelm Rowntree visited America soon after his father, Joseph Rowntree, had published his book on Temperance Reform and his brother, B. Seebohm Rowntree, his book on Poverty. Naturally J. W. Rowntree was asked if he was the author of one, or the other, or both. His reply was: "Neither; I am the son of drink and the brother of poverty."

The story *A Low Diet* is perhaps matched with this Irish one:

A Large Helping

Melview, where the Malcomsons lived in Clonmel, was a hospitable house. At Quarterly Meeting a number of Friends stopped there. One morning at breakfast a big plate of slices of ham was handed round for the guests to help themselves. One Friend, from Belfast, took the lot, saying, "Thee has helped me largely, but I'll wrassle with it."

York Meeting in Darkness

Frank Rowntree was a rare humorist. It was he and his cousin, John Wilhelm Rowntree, who in their younger days put York Monthly Meeting into darkness. The Meeting House was then ventilated by a large gas ring in the ceiling. After tea the boys had seen the caretaker coming out of a door into the roof, and when their elders had gone into the business meeting, up they went and gazed at the meeting through the hole for the gas ring. The heat of the gas jets prevented a full view, so, seeing a tap, they turned it off—and out went both gas ring and all the lights of the Meeting House.

The only other story I have out of many which could be told of Frank Rowntree is of

Caterpillar Progress

The year Theodore H. Rowntree and Katherine L. Burtt were engaged they were both officials of the York Friends' Cycling Club, an excellent institution before the days of motors. The cyclists went a run, whilst older Friends drove a shorter way in a horse-drawn wagonette, and older and younger met together in some village for tea.

Theodore H. Rowntree was the Captain of the Club and Katherine L. Burtt was Vice-Captain. Now it was laid down in the Club Rules that the Captain should ride at the head of the Club to set a suitable pace, whilst the Vice-Captain should ride at the rear to look after mishaps and stragglers.

These duties were naturally awkward for the twain, and Frank Rowntree, at the Annual Meeting held at the close of the season, said that, "The Club's progress this summer has reminded me of that species of caterpillar which goes forward by means of the head continually trying to meet the tail."

Here are a few "quick ones" given without comment.

A Yearly Meeting Report

An elderly Friend, with a still sprightly mind, wrote to her niece who was going to attend Yearly Meeting, "Write me fully, and by that I mean unsuitably."

My Host

John Salkeld, the jovial but earnest Friend, returning from a visit to New Jersey, at the beginning of the eighteenth century, said he had "breakfasted with the Lads, dined with the Lords and slept with the Hoggs," thus listing the names of the families who had entertained him.

The Pale Horse

A lawyer, meeting a Quaker on a white horse, chaffingly said, "Pray, what makes your horse look so pale in the face?" "Friend," replied the Quaker, "if thee had looked through a halter so long, thee wouldst look pale too."

The Broad-brimmed Hat

Old Isaac Sharp, the traveller, in a large and very broad-brimmed hat made specially for him, was once accosted by a street urchin with "Come out from under that hat, I know yer by yer boots."

Very like Thee

Elderly Friend at Yearly Meeting to fond mother, "I have just been talking to thy son Ted. He is very like thee, he's very plain."

The Blue Bird

William Henry Gregory met a Friend and asked him why he was absent from a recent Meeting for Discipline. He replied, "I went to the Theatre to see 'The Blue Bird.'" "What was it like?" asked W.H.G. "Oh!" was the reply, "It was just like an adjourned Quarterly Meeting."

Ascot or Epsom

At a certain Preparative Meeting, the Clerk, in reporting the removal of a Friend to Ascot, accidentally substituted Epsom, whereupon the senior elder was heard to murmur, "No, the other place."

I am indebted to I. and R. Poley's *Quaker Anecdotes* for the following:

The Quakeress at the Bank

An American girl was cashing a cheque for the first time in her life. After a question to establish her identity, the cashier was satisfied and said, as he reached for the money, "What denomination?" "Quaker" she answered.

Incorrigible

John Salkeld, an Englishman who settled in New York State, worried Friends because they felt he joked to excess. Once the elders of Meeting called and expressed their concern about his over indulgence in humour. The evening wore on. Finally he went into the kitchen and returning, said "Friends come at once—my wife is speechless." They came and found her fast asleep.

Who says Quakers aren't Tactful!

Charles S. Carter was a farmer in Chester County, Pennsylvania. One day he and his son, and a hired man were sorting potatoes in a field. To pass the time pleasantly each man in turn thought up the name of a bird, announced the initial letter and let the other two guess what bird he had in mind. When the hired man gave out R. as the initial for his bird, the Carters guessed robin, raven and rook, but these were wrong. So the hired man said, "I'll help you a little. It could be G.R." But still they couldn't guess and the hired man announced triumphantly, "Jenny Wren."

Instantly Charles Carter said "Why of course! Why didn't we think of that?"

Anglo-American Accord

Edward Grubb was visiting Rufus Jones at Haverford, U.S.A. Every night he put his shoes out to be cleaned. Since there was no one employed for that purpose in the Jones house, Rufus himself cleaned them. As he was leaving, Edward Grubb said, "Here is a dollar. Will you give it to the boy who cleans the boots?" Rufus Jones tactfully accepted the money saying, "I will see that he gets it."

Whilst the garb of the Quakeress was usually grey, the last three in Quaker garb in York Meeting were Elizabeth Gurney Dimsdale in dove-coloured grey, Emma Briggs in a dull brown and Jemima Spence (a widow) in black. The last is concerned in Roger Clark's story:

A Tale of Friends' Bonnets

Jemima Spence was an elder of the rigid old school, a tall, commanding and very broad figure, dressed in the plainest of black from head to foot, an immense and solid black Friend's bonnet, a large face and a brick red complexion. I remember seeing her embrace a Friend in the yard, also in a Friend's bonnet, but with a much smaller face: it was an excellent illustration of the verb "to telescope."

Well Matched

In P. H. Emden's *Quakers in Commerce* there is this story:

Bryant & May, the founders of the match firm, were Quakers. One day a Bryant of the younger generation was driving a coach and four in Hyde Park. "What do you think of Bryant's team?", an onlooker was asked. He quickly replied, "I think it is well matched and Bryant looks very striking on the box."

Another business story, which concerns my father is his

Change of Business

William Sessions was apprenticed to a grocer. In 1865 he purchased the stationery and printing business which still bears his name. A witty Retreat patient came in to congratulate the young man on becoming the owner of a business and as he was departing flashed out this excellent double pun: "Well, William Sessions, I hope thy business will not be stationary, but grow, sir."

To leave business we have the story of

A Quaker Party

William and Annie had no children. They gave an annual party to the young people of the Meeting. William enjoyed the young people and the games. Annie thought it a somewhat frivolous evening which might have been turned to better account.

At one of these parties William was called downstairs to see a business visitor. Annie seized on his absence to have a period of devotion. Back came William, two stairs at a time, glad to be rid of an untimely visitor, and eager for more fun and games.

He burst into the room, mistook the devotion, and cheerily exclaimed, "What! clumps again, clumps again." What bedroom lecture Annie gave to William that night is not known!

For those who do not know "clumps," may I add it is a group game, where one from each group goes out to decide on a word or object. Each then returns to another group than their own, and must answer only "yes" or "no" to questions, in the manner of "Twenty Questions" on the Radio. The group first guessing the right answer wins and all who have gone out join the winning group. Naturally each group or clump kneel closely together, the better to hear question and answer.

Did He ?

George and Priscilla had moved into a new house and Priscilla was showing a visitor round. As this feature and that was noted it was always with an "I decided," so that the visitor began to wonder where the husband came in. She was therefore relieved when a door was opened with the remark, "This is the library; here George reigns supreme." The visitor looked in and the first thing which caught her eye was a sewing machine on George's desk.

A Compliment to his Hostess

Bevan Braithwaite, in his day so weighty a Friend that he was sometimes called "The Pope," had a slight stutter. He had been visiting a Meeting and had been taken slightly ill. His hostess had looked

after him kindly and efficiently and he was grateful
to her for this extra trouble. As he bade good-bye to
his host at the station, he said with his slight stutter,
"Thy wife is indeed a ba-boon."

Candles at a Conference

In the early days of York's electric light an important Conference on the Ministry was held at the
Meeting House. The light failed and the door-keepers
rushed out to buy candles for the use of the Clerks
at the table and afterwards supplied them to groups
who were taking notes. Looked down upon from the
gallery the scene was picturesque. The dimly lighted
Meeting House with groups of earnest faces gathered
round the candles, half lit up and half in twilight,
was a scene to be remembered.

William Edward Turner was speaking at the time
the lights failed and he went on undisturbed. It is
doubtful indeed if he knew, for because of his defec-
tive eyesight he always spoke with his eyes shut. He
was staying with Maria Richardson at Cherry Hill,
just across the river from the Meeting House, and
reached by Skeldergate Bridge, which was sometimes
raised to let river traffic through. As W.E.T.'s eyesight
was not good he was warned of this. He related this
experience at dinner one evening:

York and its Bridges

William Edward Turner had left the Conference
early, not feeling quite well and unfortunately turned
right instead of left. Approaching in the twilight the

solid stone structure of Ouse Bridge, he remembered the warning that the bridge might be raised, so asked a passing workman to take him over lest he fell in the river. Wonderingly the man complied. When across, W.E.T. found something was wrong and suggested going back to the Meeting House, from whence he thought he could find his way. Back the man took him, over Ouse Bridge, along to the Meeting House and so over Skeldergate Bridge, and to Maria Richardson's house. W.E.T. thanked the working man warmly for the great trouble he had taken and received the unexpected reply, "Dean't mention it, sir, dean't mention it. I've been drunk mysen."

We pass from supposition about drink to fact in the next story of:

The Ginger Beer

Dr. Bedford Pierce, Alfred Taylor and another Friend, all Temperance speakers, were walking on the Yorkshire Moors. The day was hot and they were thirsty, so they stopped at an Inn. The friend wishing to repay in some small way his Yorkshire hosts, rushed ahead to order the ginger beer. This he did somewhat breathlessly and with a slight stutter. The refreshment proved thirst-quenching so another glassful for each was ordered. The friend insisted on paying, but the price seemed stiff, and so Alfred Taylor, not liking to see his visitor overcharged, said it seemed rather a lot for ginger beer. "Ginger beer, indeed" said the landlord, this gentleman ordered 'gin and ginger beer.' " The fresh air and the unaccustomed gin made them realize they were at least 'merry,' so they decided they could not go the short way home, but must walk off the effects of what they had drunk, even although this made them late for dinner.

Richard Westrop had been a clergyman, and after joining Friends, still retained his clerical soft hat, hence the following story:

Brother Richard

Richard Westrop came in by an early morning train. He had had a hurried breakfast and decided to go to the Refreshment Room on York station to have a glass of milk. He was also bothered by a piece of grit from the engine in his eye. When he tasted his milk he found something stronger had been put into it. He remonstrated with the girl, who replied, "That's what you ordered." "No." said Brother Richard firmly, "I only ordered milk." "Now look here," said the girl, "when a parson comes in and orders milk and gives me a wink, what else is he ordering but what I've given you." Brother Richard told her about the grit in his eye, only to be sharply reminded not to order milk again when he had anything in his eye!

The next story can be left to speak for itself.

Keeping a Pig

At a meeting of the National Council of Adult Schools the discussion had been warm on the subject of social work in our Schools. A delegate from Bridlington rose to make the point that what some called "social work" was religious in the fullest sense.

He elaborated with much energy and fine phrases and finally said, "For instance, we have a man in our School who had a great superfluity of flesh; he was a very heavy drinker and a betting man. We wondered how to help him. We got him an allotment and a pig, and, what with working the allotment and trundling food for the pig, he began to get thinner. He left off drinking and gambling and became quite a changed character. Now you may call that social work, but I call it religious." The speaker sat down amid applause, for he had made a good point and made it well.

Then rose Joseph B. Braithwaite, whose portly form was made more evident by his leaning against the table. Before he could speak, his brother William Charles, by his side, looked up and asked, "Joseph, dost thou keep a pig?" It was a long time before the meeting could go on with the business, but then J.B.B. proceeded as if nothing had happened.

A story of John Bright on a fishing holiday in Ireland is worth relating:

A Fishing Story

John Bright and George Peabody, whilst staying at Castle Connell, decided to spend a day at Killaboe fishing on Lough Derg. Landing from the boat they did not know how much to pay, so asked a policeman standing near. He suggested 7/6d. George Peabody handed the boatman three half-crowns. Holding them in his hand and looking at them quizzingly, the boatman said, "Begorra they call ye Mishther Paybody but I say ye're Mishther Pay nobody."

The Friends' Relief Service in the last war had its lighter moments, and here are some of them picked from its Journal *The Star*

In the Day's Work of the F.R.S.

Letter received by the Alien's Section: "I have read several times in your papers an advertisement from Oats Quaker Ltd. Is this Company a branch of your Mission?"

In a letter from a parallel organization: "As you probably know I have been pulled into the supply picture for Central Europe."

From an old Mount Waltham time-table:
"10-55 a.m. What think ye of God?
2-30 p.m. Visit to Hampstead Cleansing Station."

Showing the F.R.S. Film

Question 8 on the form sent out about film booking asks, "Can you provide transport from the nearest station to the hall?" One answer was, "We have a wheelbarrow and a little trolley (same size)"

An applicant asked, "Does it need more than a small church hall and a sheet?"

Extracts from Service Team Reports

"Great efforts have been made to provide materials for artificial teeth, but these have not borne any fruit yet."

"Among the individual cases brought to our notice was that of a young man in difficult straits; being rather lonely, he had advertised for a wife and had

had twenty-four replies. Meanwhile the F.R.S. team was giving him temporary help.''

The absence of outward ritual in a Quaker Meeting is responsible for some regarding Friends as a very worthy body of people, but not as a religious denomination. This is brought out in the following story of:

The New Matron

"A new matron (Margaret Haughton) had been appointed to Limerick Hospital. I heard some women discussing the matter. 'An' what is her religion?' was the natural Irish question. Another said, 'Av course a protestant, becas the House Surgeon is a catholic.' 'But what kind of a protestant?' asked a third. To which the second replied 'Sure they say she is a Quaker.' At this there seemed to be general agreement with another who said, 'Och thin! it's all right. The Quakers have no religion!''

Arnold S. Rowntree loved a good story and he much enjoyed telling this one against himself.

Bilers

Arnold S. Rowntree was staying at the Inn at Byland Abbey, the landlady of which was a great Yorkshire character, known as "George" or "Georgie." She was sorting some of the poultry which had been killed for market into chickens and old hens for boiling. Some remark as to ages cropped up and "George" turned to Arnold and said, "Aye, you and me be bilers (boilers).''

The Quaker journal *The Friend* printed a good story against itself.

Unusually Comic

A lady enquired at her local newsagent for *The Friend*. The answer was, "No madam, the Comics have not come in yet."

I include this story out of my own experience because of the excellent repartee, coming so suddenly and unexpectedly out of the darkness of a winter's night by the roadside.

Give him a kiss, loike

All day I had been round the polling booths and Committee Rooms of the Thirsk and Malton Division and about half-an-hour before the poll closed, I came to a little railway hamlet where some voters were waiting for a conveyance. They piled into the car, there was a shout and a woman came running out of the darkness. She was being hastily bundled into the car, when she suddenly backed out, exclaiming, "Wait a minute, I've niver voted. What do I do, Jim?" "Oh! it's easy, they give ye a paper wi' Sessions and Turton on, thee put a cross against name o' Sessions." "Wot, give 'im a kiss, loike," said the woman. Quick as a flash came out of the darkness, "Aye, that's it, an' it's t'only kiss 'is wife wean't mind."

Here is another story of the countryside:

As the Dales folk see us

The usual commentary on the Society of Friends by the North Riding Dales folk is: "Quakers is queer folks; they marries theirsens, and they buries theirsens."

CHAPTER X

QUAKER HUMOROUS POETRY

PICKLED COCKLES

This poem of Mary E. Manners gives a delightful description of olden Quaker ways. It is perhaps the best humorous Quaker poem which has been written. It was first published in the "Boys Own Paper" from whom I have kindly received permission to reprint it here.

In the old-fashion "Friendly" days,
    When Quaker garb and Quaker ways
Had not died out—when Quaker phrase
Was heard in every Friendly greeting,
And not merely reserved for "Preparative Meeting:"
        When old and young
        Used the Quaker tongue,
        Said "thee" and "thou,"
        Declined to bow,
        And thought a song
        Most improper and wrong;
In the days we love—to hear about
(They were less amusing to live in, no doubt),
There dwelt just outside a suburban town
A dear old Friend named Tabitha Brown.

Now Tabitha Brown was clad always
In the softest of drabs and most dove-like of greys;
With the whitest of caps on her silver hair,
And aprons and mittens and all "to compare;"
While out of doors she was just the same,—

Most spotless, quiet, and free from blame;
Her shawl was neatly folded in,
And kept in its place by a white-headed pin;
The sweet placid face, neath the silver hair
(Showing lines of sorrow, but none of care),
Looked out from a bonnet quaint and shady,—
She was what one might call a real "Quaker Lady."
Thy excuse, gentle spirit—I apprehend
Thou wert what's better still, a true "Woman
    Friend."

Tabitha Brown was well skilled in the arts
Of making pies, and puddings, and tarts;
Of pickling, preserving, and baking, and brewing,
Of boiling and roasting, and frying and stewing,
        Cheese-pressing and churning—
        In all sorts of learning
Connected with thrifty household ways,
Tabitha Brown was above all praise.
In fact there was nothing she couldn't make,
From a whole-meal loaf to a wedding cake!

        While for dusting and rubbing,
For swilling and mopping, for sweeping with brooms,
For turning the furniture out of the rooms,
For shaking of beds and for beating of chairs,
For taking up carpets and cleaning the stairs;
For polishing pots, pans, dishes and kettles,
And everything else that is made of bright metals;
For leaving black beetles and spiders no peace,
For using that article termed "elbow-grease,"
Together with soap, sand, bath-brick, and blacklead,
Emery paper (or what was then used instead),

For keeping the house without spot, speck, or stain,
There never was servant like Phoebe Jane!
In short, and most boys will, I think, grasp my
     meaning,
She kept up *all the year* one perpetual "spring-
     cleaning."

Phoebe Jane was tidy and trim,
But no Quaker dress could make her look prim;
And, notwithstanding her "Friendly" gown,
She failed to resemble Tabitha Brown.
Her bonnet and shawl were just as plain,
Yet they looked somehow different on Phoebe Jane;
While rebellious curls would sometimes stray
From her cap, in a most unorthodox way,
And, though she persistently brushed them o'er,
They only curled tighter than before.
Her temper, too, was none of the best;
And if any one, either mistress or guest,
Her peculiar notions chanced to offend, she
        Her feelings expressed
        (It must be confessed)
In Quakerly speech which was not always "friendly";
And Tabitha Brown wrote these words in her Diary:
"P.J.'s heart—it is good, but her temper—is fiery."

This quiet household contained a third,—
A jackdaw, a really remarkable bird!
From the day he left his parental nest
In Quaker language he'd been addressed;
And he talked in quite as "Friendly" a strain
As Tabitha Brown or Phoebe Jane.

No schoolboy's freak
        Had e'er taught him to speak
Of "awfully jolly," or "stunning," or "fine,"
        Or to whistle sad airs
        About "oysters" and "stairs,"
And "Ehren," or "Bingen, " or "Bonn" "on the
    Rhine."
        Sedate and grave,
        He knew how to behave;
On points of decorum his feelings were sensitive;
        Friends scarce had erred
        Had they sent this bird
To the "Quarterly Meeting" as "Representative."
Tho' no doubt he would not have failed to declare
That he certainly "did not expect to be there."

But not even beneficent Quaker law
Can eradicate mischief from a jackdaw,
        And a failing bad
        He once had had
Which is common to all of his species and genus
(Pray let it be kept a secret between us)
He had not a conscience sufficiently fine
To discriminate clearly 'twixt "mine" and "thine."
        On thimbles and keys,
        Button-hooks and green peas,
        Spoons ("tables" or "teas")
        He would suddenly seize
        Without saying "please,"
And convey them to places not reached with great
    ease—
        To the tops of tall trees,

Rocked by Spring's gentle breeze.
Or to crannies thro' which your hand could not
   squeeze.
      Once, when many degrees
      Of cold made it freeze,
And Tabitha Brown 'gan to cough and to sneeze,
She sent for her doctor, the best of M.D.'s,
And this naughty jackdaw ran away with the fees.
      But 'twas long ago
      Since he'd acted so;
And Tabitha gently said, "Thee know,
We ought to have charity, Phoebe Jane;
I do not think 'twill occur again."

Now of all the receipts which Friend Brown pos-
   sessed,
She prized one more highly than the rest,
Which from mother to daughter handed down,
Had for years belonged to the race of Brown;
'Twas for pickled cockles, and Friends would declare,
When they tasted the "Monthly Meeting" fare,
That this dish was indeed beyond compare.
So though Tabitha looked with benignant eyes
On the rapid consumption of puddings and pies,
And showed, indeed, very small reserve
In the matter of marmalade and preserve,
She was somewhat "exercised in her mind,"
On entering the storeroom one morning, to find
That the jar she had thought was filled to the brim
With dainty molluscs in orderly trim,
Was in truth half empty; and in some pain
She mentioned the fact to Phoebe Jane:

"They'll not last until cockles come round again."
But Phoebe Jane was very cross,
And, as she gave her head a toss,
Replied, "I thought thee couldn't know
That the stock was getting low
                    Of pickled cockles."
Tabitha quietly withdrew,
Yet still, alas! 'tis very true
That neither mistress nor maid could guess
How day by day the store grew less,
                    Of pickled cockles.

And Phoebe Jane took it into her head
That her mistress didn't believe what she said
And remarked, as she took the breakfast up,
"I know thee think I dine and sup
                    On pickled cockles."

And, though Tabitha calmly assured her that she
Had not the least doubt of her honesty,
Phoebe still declared that she couldn't remain
If her character wasn't freed from the strain
                    Of those pickled cockles.

One afternoon it chanced that she
Was filling the little brass kettle for tea;
When, turning round, with surprise she saw,
On the ground beside her, the grave jackdaw
                    Eating pickled cockles.

The kettle falls, the waters pour
Over jackdaw, grate, and kitchen floor;

And Phoebe cries, with excited feeling,
"Ah! Friend, I see that thee've been stealing
                The pickled cockles!"

The poor jackdaw became very bald
From the dire effects of that terrible scald;
He looked a most deplorable fright,
And he never after could bear the sight
                Of pickled cockles.

For a year and a day this poor little bird
Never opened his mouth to speak a word;
At the end of that time an event occurred
Which caused his voice once more to be heard.
Tabitha Brown had a brother-in-law,
As strict a Quaker as ever you saw;
His coat was long, and his collar was straight;
You knew him at once as a "Friend of weight."
He wore a broad-brimmed beaver hat,
And rejoiced in the name of "Nathaniel Pratt."

    Now this "weighty Friend"
    Came up to attend
The famed "Yearly Meeting" of which you have
  heard,
    Which begins, so Friends say,
    "On the first Fourth day
Which follows the First day, in order the third,
    Of the Fifth month."—Pray,
    Might I venture to say
That this is rather a roundabout way
Of describing the third or fourth Wednesday in May?

'Twas First day morning, and eight or nine
Most "well-concerned Friends" had met to dine
At Tabitha Brown's. Nathaniel Pratt,
Who on the right hand of the hostess sat,
Still wore, sedately, his broad-brimmed hat;
But having thus borne his testimony
In a manner in which he stood quite alone, he
Began to think that he now was free
To consider himself at liberty
To consult his comfort in some degree;
So he took off his hat, and exposed to view
A massive head, which, I assure you,
Might have served as a model for Giunta of Pisa,
    Who loved to paint
    A benevolent saint
As bald—as bald as Julius Caesar,
With a halo instead of the laurel rare
Which the Senate permitted the latter to wear
To conceal the scarcity of his hair!
(For further particulars see Lemprière.)
The jackdaw, whom nobody thought of heeding,
Took a lively interest in the proceeding;
And though he had never studied geology,
And had no acquaintance with natural laws,
It was plain to this cleverest of jackdaws,
That effect, as a rule, must proceed from cause.
Then, not stopping to make the slightest apology,
    With a knowing air
    He perched on the chair
Of the "weighty Friend" who had lost his hair,
    And exclaimed in his ear
    In tones loud and clear,

And yet with a touch of pity sincere
(Inspired, no doubt, by a fellow feeling),
"Ah, Friend I see that THEE' VE been stealing
                              The pickled cockles."

MORAL

Don't steal Pickled Cockles—fresh ones are not dear
And if in your mind you are not quite clear
Concerning the pickling, look out the receipt on
Page three-ninety-one of the late Mrs. Beeton.
Thirdly, and lastly—I speak with due cause—
I would certainly strongly advise you to pause
Before you put faith in the best of Jackdaws!

A LITTLE MAIDEN'S GOWN

A little Quaker maiden, with dimpled cheek and chin,
Before an ancient mirror stood, and viewed her form
    within.
She wore a gown of sober grey, a cape demure and
    prim,
With only simple fold and hem, yet dainty, neat, and
    trim;
Her bonnet, too, was grey and stiff; its only line of
    grace
Was in the lace, so soft and white, that framed her
    rosy face.
Quoth she, "Oh, how I hate this hat! I hate this gown
    and cape,
I do wish all my clothes were not of such outlandish
    shape.
The children passing by to school have ribbons in
    their hair,

The girl next door wears blue; oh, dear, if I could dare,
I know what I should like to do" (the words were whispered low,
Lest such tremendous heresy should reach her aunts below).
Calmly reading in the parlour sat the good aunts, Faith and Peace,
Little dreaming how rebellious throbbed the heart of their young niece.
All their prudent, humble teaching wilfully she cast aside,
And, her mind now fully conquered by sad vanity and pride,
She, with trembling heart and fingers, on a hassock sat her down,
And this little Quaker sinner sewed a tuck into her gown.
"Little Patience, art thou ready? Fifth-day meeting time has come,
Mercy Jones and Goodman Elder with his wife have left their home."
'Twas Aunt Faith's sweet voice that called her, and the naughty little maid,
Gliding down the dark old stairway, hoped their notice to evade,
Keeping slyly in their shadow as they went out at the door,
Ah, never little Quakeress a guiltier conscience bore,
Dear Aunt Faith walked looking upward, all her thoughts were pure and holy,
And Aunt Peace walked gazing downward, with a humble mind and lowly,

But "tuck, tuck," chirped the sparrows at the little
    maiden's side,
And in passing Farmer Watson's where the barn
    door opened wide,
Every sound that issued from it, every grunt and
    every cluck,
Seemed to her affrighted fancy like "a tuck," "a
    tuck," "a tuck."
In Meeting, Goodman Elder spoke of pride and
    vanity,
Whilst all the Friends seemed looking round that
    dreadful tuck to see;
How it swelled in its proportion, till it seemed to fill
    the air,
And the heart of little Patience grew heavier with
    her care.
Oh, the glad relief to her when, prayers and exhor-
    tations ended,
Behind her two good aunties her homeward way she
    wended.
The pomp and vanities of life she'd seized with
    eager arms,
And deeply she had tasted of the world's alluring
    charms,
Yea, to the dregs had drained them, and only this to
    find,
All was vanity of spirit and vexation of the mind.
So, repentant, saddened, humbled, on her hassock
    she sat down,
And this little Quaker sinner ripped the tuck out of
    her gown.

ANON.

THE GENERAL ADVICES IN RHYME

The General Advices are read in each Quaker Meeting once in each year. This humorous version is based on the Advices prior to the revision of 1928.

> Let thy accounts be kept with care
> See that there be no errors there.
> Do not defer till thou art ill,
> The due completion of thy will.
>
> Also throughout thy time of health
> Beware accumulating wealth,
> Thy surplus thousands give away
> To those who lack the means to pay.
>
> By acting thus thou wilt ensure
> The heartfelt blessings of the poor,
> And thou thyself wilt evermore
> Be blessed in basket and in store.
>
> Be strictly honest in thy dealings,
> Discouraging all greedy feelings;
> And do not speculation choose,
> Or thou wilt very likely lose.
>
> So therefore without more preamble,
> We recommend thee not to gamble,
> Or thou may'st wish, when all is spent,
> Thou'd rested safe with 3%.

We trust that thou wilt do thy best
That games of chance may be suppressed;
Nor would the Meeting feel annoyed,
If billiard tables were destroyed.

All places of diversion shun,
Except the tea and modest bun;
Also avoid inflicting pain
By sports denominated vain,

On furniture and dress expend
No more than doth become a Friend;
In all thy actions lay aside
Whatever tends to worldly pride.

Seek after Friends of modest worth,
Rather than great ones of the earth;
And (if allowed to by thy wife)
Aim ever at the simple life.

Let living plain and thinking high
Be the good rule thou livest by,
And, if thou should'st prepare a feast,
Ask not the greatest but the least.

So when thy earthly course is run,
And all thy work below is done,
By living thus thou yet may'st end
A tolerably consistent Friend.

JAMES I'ANSON, Darlington

It is strange that authors greet their readers at the beginning of a book by Preface, Foreword and Introduction, but never say farewell. An Appendix or two, an Addendum, or an Index form their only parting.

May I break this custom, and say with Friendly greeting: Dear Reader, I hope thou hast enjoyed my book. If thou hast found some of the stories were known to thee, may these not prove to be the fruits of AESCULUS HIPPOCASTANUM*, but rather of* CASTANEA SATIVA,* and therefore palatable.*

Farewell.

---

*AESCULUS HIPPOCASTANUM : the Horse Chestnut;
CASTANEA SATIVA : the Sweet Chestnut.